GCSE Success

Revision Guide

Mathematics Foundation

Fiona C. Mapp

Contents

Number

		Revised
Numbers	4	☐
Positive and negative numbers	6	☐
Working with numbers	8	☐
Fractions	10	☐
Decimals	12	☐
Rounding	14	☐
Percentages 1	16	☐
Percentages 2	18	☐
Equivalents	20	☐
Using a calculator	21	☐
Approximating and checking calculations	22	☐
Ratio	24	☐
Indices	26	☐
Practice questions	28	☐

Algebra

		Revised
Algebra 1	30	☐
Algebra 2	32	☐
Equations 1	34	☐
Equations 2	36	☐
Patterns, sequences and inequalities	38	☐
Straight line graphs	40	☐
Curved graphs	42	☐
Interpreting graphs	44	☐
Practice questions	46	☐

Shape, space and measures

	Revised
Shapes 48	☐
Solids 50	☐
Symmetry 52	☐
Constructions 53	☐
Angles 54	☐
Bearings and scale drawings 56	☐
Transformations 1 58	☐
Transformations 2 60	☐
Loci and coordinates 62	☐
Pythagoras' theorem 64	☐
Measures and measurement 1 65	☐
Measures and measurement 2 68	☐
Area of 2D shapes 70	☐
Volume of 3D shapes 72	☐
Practice questions 74	☐

Handling data

	Revised
Collecting data 76	☐
Representing data 78	☐
Scatter diagrams and correlation 80	☐
Averages 1 82	☐
Averages 2 84	☐
Probability 1 86	☐
Probability 2 88	☐
Practice questions 90	☐

Answers 92
Index 96

Numbers

Square roots and cube roots

Taking the square root is the opposite of squaring. $\sqrt{}$ is the square root sign.

For example, $\sqrt{25} = \pm 5$ since $5^2 = 25$, or $(-5)^2 = 25$.

Taking the cube root is the opposite of cubing. $\sqrt[3]{}$ is the cube root sign.

For example, $\sqrt[3]{8} = 2$ since $2^3 = 8$.

Squares and cubes

Square numbers
Anything to the **power 2** is a **square**. For example, $6^2 = 6 \times 6 = 36$ (six squared).
Square numbers include:

1	4	9	16	25	36	49	64	81	100	...
(1 × 1)	(2 × 2)	(3 × 3)	(4 × 4)	(5 × 5)	(6 × 6)	(7 × 7)	(8 × 8)	(9 × 9)	(10 × 10)	

Square numbers can be illustrated by drawing squares. You need to know up to 15^2.

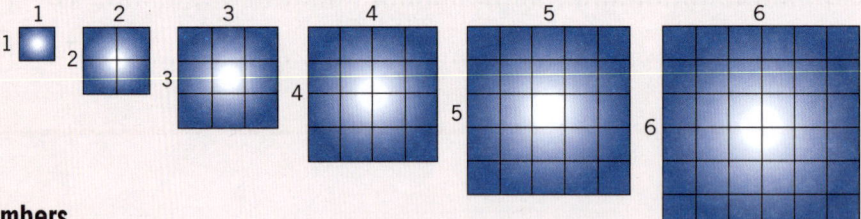

Cube numbers
Anything to the **power 3** is a **cube**. For example, $5^3 = 5 \times 5 \times 5 = 125$ (five cubed).
Cube numbers include:

1	8	27	64	125	216 ...
(1 × 1 × 1)	(2 × 2 × 2)	(3 × 3 × 3)	(4 × 4 × 4)	(5 × 5 × 5)	(6 × 6 × 6)

Cube numbers can be illustrated by drawing cubes:

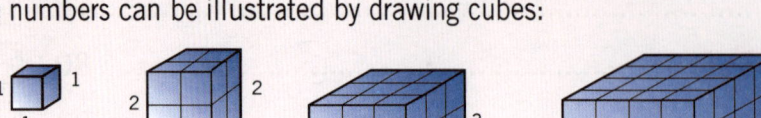

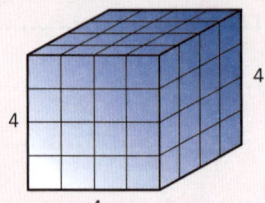

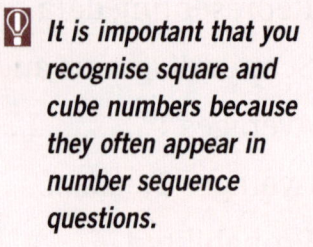

💡 *It is important that you recognise square and cube numbers because they often appear in number sequence questions.*

Reciprocals

The **reciprocal** of a number $\frac{a}{x}$ is $\frac{x}{a} (= x \div a)$. Multiplying a number by its reciprocal always gives 1. Zero does not have a reciprocal.

Examples
- The reciprocal of $\frac{2}{3}$ is $\frac{3}{2}$.
- The reciprocal of 4 is $\frac{1}{4}$ because 4 is the same as $\frac{4}{1}$.
- To find the reciprocal of $1\frac{2}{3}$, first put it in the form $\frac{a}{x}$ ($1\frac{2}{3} = \frac{5}{3}$), then invert it to give $\frac{3}{5}$.

Factors and primes

Factors
These are whole numbers that **divide exactly** into another number. To find all the factors of a number, start at 1 and divide by each number in turn. For example, the factors of 20 are 1, 2, 4, 5, 10 and 20. Factors can be split up into factor pairs.

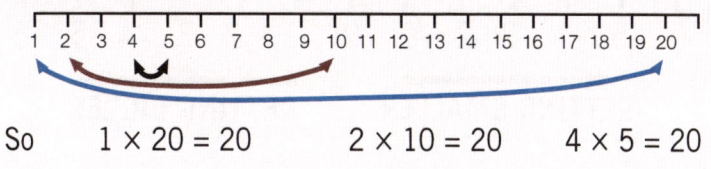

```
1  2  3  4  5  6  7  8  9  10  11  12  13  14  15  16  17  18  19  20
```

So $\quad 1 \times 20 = 20 \qquad 2 \times 10 = 20 \qquad 4 \times 5 = 20$

Prime numbers
These are numbers which have only two factors, **1 and itself**. Note that 1 is **not** a prime number. The prime numbers up to 20 are 2, 3, 5, 7, 11, 13, 17 and 19.

Prime factors

These are factors which are prime.
All numbers, except prime numbers, can be written as products of their prime factors.

Example
The diagram below (a **prime factor tree**) shows the prime factors of 360.
- Divide 360 by its first prime factor, 2.
- Divide 180 by its first prime factor, 2.
- Keep on going until the final number is prime.

As a product of its prime factors,
360 can be written as:
$2 \times 2 \times 2 \times 3 \times 3 \times 5 = 360$
or $2^3 \times 3^2 \times 5 = 360$
in **index notation** (using powers).

Highest common factor (HCF)
The largest factor that two numbers have in common is called the **HCF**.

Example
Find the HCF of 84 and 360.
- First write the numbers as products of their prime factors.
  $84 = 2 \times 2 \times 3 \times 7$
  $360 = 2 \times 2 \times 2 \times 3 \times 3 \times 5$
- Ring the factors they have in common.
- These give the HCF = $2 \times 2 \times 3 = 12$

Lowest common multiple (LCM)
The **LCM** is the lowest number which is a multiple of two numbers.

Example
Find the LCM of 6 and 8.
- First write the numbers as products of their prime factors.
- $8 = 2 \times 2 \times 2$
- $6 = 2 \times 3$
- 8 and 6 have a common prime factor of 2. So it is only included once.
- The LCM of 6 and 8 is $2 \times 2 \times 2 \times 3 = 24$

KEY TERMS
Make sure you understand these terms before moving on!
- square number
- cube number
- reciprocal
- factor
- prime number
- HCF
- LCM

QUICK TEST

1. List the prime numbers up to 20.
2. Find the HCF and LCM of 24 and 60.
3. Find: a) $\sqrt{64}$ b) $\sqrt[3]{216}$
4. Write down the reciprocals of:
   a) $\frac{9}{12}$ b) $\frac{x}{p}$

Positive and negative numbers

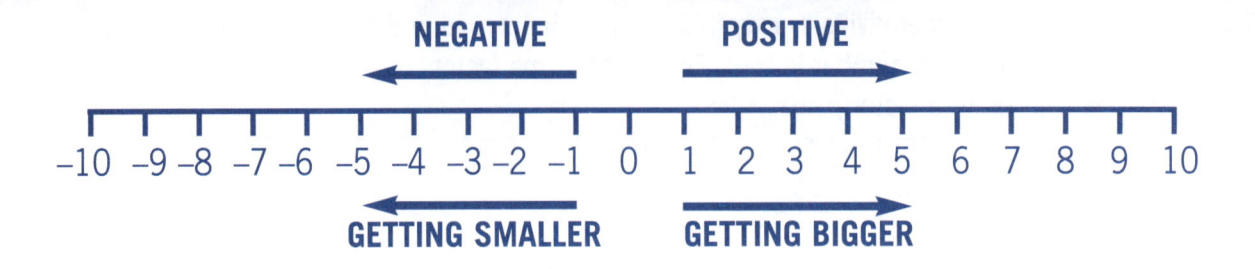

NEGATIVE ← | → POSITIVE

–10 –9 –8 –7 –6 –5 –4 –3 –2 –1 0 1 2 3 4 5 6 7 8 9 10

← GETTING SMALLER | GETTING BIGGER →

Directed numbers

These are numbers which may be **positive** or **negative**.
Positive numbers are above zero, negative numbers are below zero.

Examples
–10 is smaller than –8.   –10 < –8
–4 is bigger than –8.   –4 > –8
2 is bigger than –6.   2 > –6

Directed numbers are often seen on the weather forecast in winter. Quite often the **temperature** is below 0.
Aberdeen is the coldest on this forecast map at –8°C.
London is 6°C warmer than Manchester.

-8 Aberdeen
-4 Manchester
2 London

Integers

The **integers** are the set of numbers {. . . –3, –2, –1, 0, 1, 2, 3, . . .}.
When referring to integers, the term **integral value** is used.
A number that is **non-integral** is not an integer.

Multiplying and dividing directed numbers

Multiply and divide the numbers as normal.
Then find the sign for the answer using these rules:

- two **like** signs (both + or both –) give a positive answer.
- two **unlike** signs (one + and the other –) give a negative answer.

(+) × (+) = +
(−) × (−) = +
(+) × (−) = −
(−) × (+) = −
(+) ÷ (+) = +
(−) ÷ (−) = +
(+) ÷ (−) = −
(−) ÷ (+) = −

Examples
–6 × (+4) = –24   –12 ÷ (–3) = 4
–6 × (–3) = 18   20 ÷ (–4) = –5

You need to remember the rules of multiplication/division.
You will find these laws useful when multiplying out brackets in algebra.

Adding and subtracting directed numbers

Example
The temperature at 6 a.m. was −5°C. By 10 a.m. it had risen 8 degrees.
So the new temperature was 3°C.

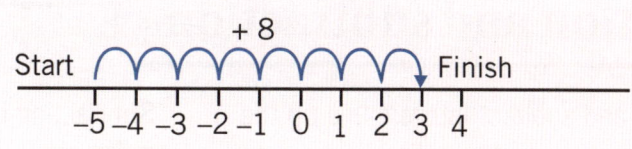

Example
Find the value of −2 − 4.

*This represents the **sign** of the number. Start at −2.* → −2 − 4

*This represents the operation of **subtraction**. Move 4 places to the left.*

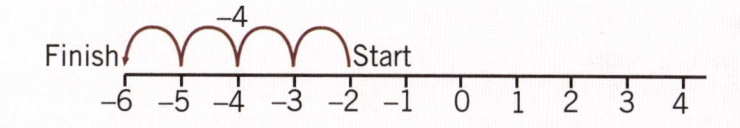

So −2 − 4 = −6

When the number to be added (or subtracted) is **negative**, the normal direction of movement is **reversed**.

Example   −4 − (−3) is the same as −4 + 3 = −1
The negative changes the direction.   Move 3 places to the right.

When two (+) or two (−) signs are together, these rules are used:

+(+) → +
−(−) → + } **like** signs give a **plus**,

+(−) → −
−(+) → − } **unlike** signs give a **minus**.

Examples
−6 + (−2) = −6 − 2 = −8   −2 − (+6) = −2 − 6 = −8
4 − (−3) = 4 + 3 = 7   9 + (−3) = 9 − 3 = 6

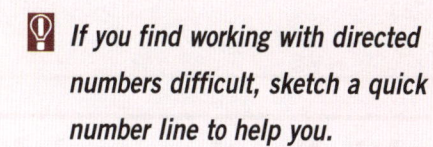

💡 *If you find working with directed numbers difficult, sketch a quick number line to help you.*

Negative numbers on a calculator

The [+/−] or [(−)] key on the calculator gives a **negative** number.
For example, to get −6, press [6] [+/−] or [(−)] [6].

Example
−4 − (−2) = −2
is keyed in the calculator like this:

[4] [+/−] [−] [2] [+/−] [=]
 sign operation sign

Make sure you know how to enter negative numbers in **your** calculator.

KEY TERMS

Make sure you understand these terms before moving on!
- directed number
- integer

QUICK TEST

1. If the temperature was −12°C at 2 a.m. and it rose by 15 degrees by 11 a.m., what was the temperature at 11 a.m.?

2. Work these out, without a calculator.
   a) −2 − (−6)   b) −9 + (−7)   c) −2 × 6
   d) −9 + (−3)   e) −20 ÷ (−4)   f) −18 ÷ (−3)
   g) 4 − (−3)   h) −7 + (−3)   i) −9 × −4

POSITIVE AND NEGATIVE NUMBERS — Number

Working with numbers

Addition and subtraction

When you add and subtract integers line up the place values one on top of the other.

Example
Add 5263 + 398

```
 5263        Line up the numbers first.
  398 +      Add the units, then the 10s, etc.
 5661
   1 1       The one is carried here into the tens column.
```

This addition can be checked mentally by using **partitioning**. An empty number line can help.

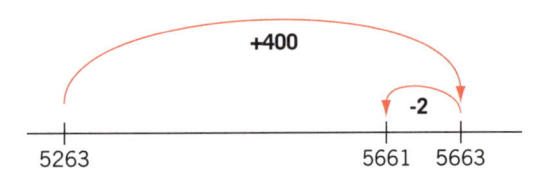

```
       +400
   5263      5661 5663
                -2
```

Subtracting is also known as finding the **difference**.

Example
Find the difference between 2791 and 363.

```
 27⁸⁹¹1      In the units column, subtracting 3 from 1
  363 −      won't work, so borrow 10 from the next
 2428        column. The 9 becomes an 8 and the 1
             becomes 11.
```

Compensation can be used to check the answer, by adding or subtracting too much and then compensating.

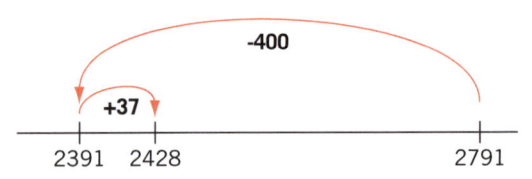

```
              −400
      +37
   2391 2428              2791
```

Multiplication and division by 10, 100, 1000

To **multiply** by 10, 100, 1000, etc., move the digits one, two, three, etc. places to the left and put in zeros if necessary.

Examples

6.3 × 10 = 63   Move the digits one place to the left.

47 × 10 = 470   Put in a zero, moving digits one place to the left.

17.4 × 100 = 1740   Move the digits two places to the left.

68 × 100 = 6800   Put in two zeros, moving digits two places to the left.

To **divide** by 10, 100, 1000, etc., move the digits one, two, three, etc. places to the right.

Examples
17.6 ÷ 10 = 1.76   74 ÷ 100 = 0.74
19.6 ÷ 1000 = 0.0196

When multiplying by multiples of 10 (e.g. 20, 30, 700), the same rules apply, except you multiply the numbers first then move the digits to the left.

Examples
60 × 30 = 60 × 3 × 10 = 180 × 10 = 1800
5.2 × 20 = 5.2 × 2 × 10 = 10.4 × 10 = 104

When dividing by multiples of 10, the same rules apply, except you divide the numbers and then move the digits to the right.

Examples
6000 ÷ 30 = 6000 ÷ 3 ÷ 10 = 2000 ÷ 10 = 200
6.3 ÷ 30 = 6.3 ÷ 3 ÷ 10 = 2.1 ÷ 10 = 0.21

Long multiplication

When you multiply two or more numbers together you are finding the **product**.

Example
A tin of soup costs 64p. Work out the cost of 127 tins of soup.

Cost = 127 × 64

```
   127
    64 ×
   508      Step 1: 127 × 4
  7620 +    Step 2: 127 × 60
  8128      Step 3: 508 + 7620
```

Cost = 8128p or £81.28

Alternatively, you can use a 'grid' method.

×	100	20	7	
60	6000	1200	420	→ 7620
4	400	80	28	→ 508 +
				8128

= £81.28

Long division

A pencil costs 27p. Samuel has £3.66 to spend. What is the maximum number of pencils he can buy? How much change will he have left over?

```
     13
27 ) 366
     27
     96
     81
     15
```

Step 1: 27 goes into 36 once, put down 1
Step 2: place 27 below 36
Step 3: subtract 27 from 36 (get 9)
Step 4: bring down the 6
Step 5: divide 27 into 96, put down the 3
Step 6: 96 − 81 = remainder 15

Samuel can buy 13 pencils and he will have 15p left over.

The method of **chunking** can also be used when dividing. Always try to estimate the answer to your division.

```
27 ) 366
     270   − 27 × 10
      96
      81   − 27 × 3
      15
```

366 ÷ 27 = 10 + 3, remainder 15
       = 13 pencils and 15p left over

In this example, 27 is the **divisor**, 13 is the **quotient** and the **remainder** is 15.

KEY TERMS

Make sure you understand these terms before moving on!
- difference
- product
- divisor
- quotient
- remainder

QUICK TEST

Answer the following questions.

1. a) 479 + 698   b) 379 − 147
   c) 287 × 6   d) 5) 1375

2. 427 × 48

3. 49) 1813

4. a) 16.4 × 10   b) 8.9 × 100
   c) 37 × 1000   d) 97 ÷ 1000

5. The cost of a trip is £15.65. If Ms Kier collects £657.30, how many people are going on the trip? Work this out without using a calculator.

WORKING WITH NUMBERS — Number

Fractions

A fraction is a part of a whole.
The top number is the *numerator*.
The bottom number is the *denominator*.
A fraction like $\frac{4}{5}$ is called a *proper fraction*.
A fraction like $\frac{24}{17}$ is called an *improper fraction*.
$2\frac{1}{2}$ is called a mixed number.

$\frac{4}{5}$ means 4 parts out of 5.

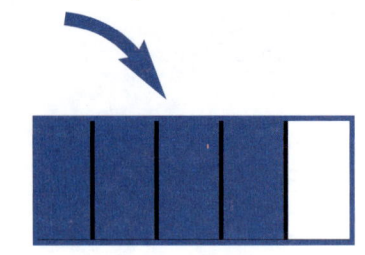

Equivalent fractions

Example
These are fractions which have the same value.

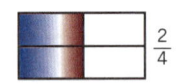

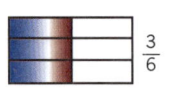

$\frac{1}{2}$ $\frac{2}{4}$ $\frac{3}{6}$ $\frac{4}{8}$

From the diagrams it can be seen that $\frac{1}{2} = \frac{2}{4} = \frac{3}{6} = \frac{4}{8}$.

They are **equivalent fractions**. Fractions can be changed to their equivalents by **multiplying** or **dividing** both the numerator and denominator by the same amount.

Examples
1. Change $\frac{5}{7}$ to its equivalent fraction with a denominator of 28. 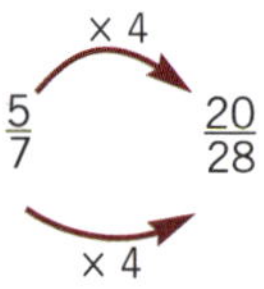
   Multiply top and bottom by 4.
   So $\frac{5}{7}$ is equivalent to $\frac{20}{28}$.

   $\frac{5}{7} \xrightarrow{\times 4} \frac{20}{28}$

2. Change $\frac{40}{60}$ to its equivalent fraction with a denominator of 3. 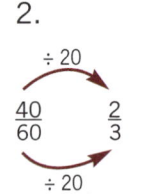
   Divide top and bottom by 20.
   So $\frac{40}{60}$ is equivalent to $\frac{2}{3}$.
   $\frac{40}{60} = \frac{2}{3}$ in its simplest form.

   $\frac{40}{60} \xrightarrow{\div 20} \frac{2}{3}$

Using the fraction key on the calculator

$\boxed{a\%}$ is the fraction key on the calculator.

Example
$\frac{12}{18}$ is keyed in as $\boxed{1}\boxed{2}\boxed{a\%}\boxed{1}\boxed{8}$. This is displayed as $\boxed{12\rfloor 18}$ or $\boxed{12\text{-}18}$.
The calculator will automatically cancel down fractions when the $\boxed{=}$ key is pressed.
For example, $\frac{12}{18}$ becomes $\boxed{2\rfloor 3}$ or $\boxed{2\text{-}3}$. This means two-thirds.

A display of $\boxed{1\rfloor 4\rfloor 9}$ means $1\frac{4}{9}$. If you now press $\boxed{\text{shift}}\boxed{a\%}$,
it converts back to an improper fraction, $\boxed{13\rfloor 9}$.

Multiplication and division of fractions

When multiplying and dividing fractions, first write out whole or mixed numbers as improper fractions.

Example

$\frac{2}{9} \times \frac{4}{7} = \frac{2 \times 4}{9 \times 7} = \frac{8}{63}$ ← Multiply numerators together
← Multiply denominators together

Change a division into a multiplication by turning the second fraction upside down and multiplying both fractions together; that is, **multiply by the reciprocal**.

Example

$\frac{7}{9} \div \frac{12}{18} = \frac{7}{9} \times \frac{18}{12}$ Take the **reciprocal** of the **second fraction**.

$= \frac{126}{108} = 1\frac{1}{6}$ Rewrite the answer as a mixed number.

Addition and subtraction of fractions

These examples show the basic principles of adding and subtracting fractions.

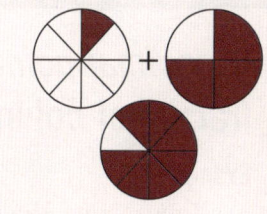

Example
$\frac{1}{8} + \frac{3}{4}$

- First make the denominators the same: $\frac{3}{4} \xrightarrow{\times 2} \frac{6}{8}$

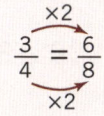

  $\frac{3}{4}$ is **equivalent** to $\frac{6}{8}$.

$= \frac{1}{8} + \frac{6}{8}$

- Replace $\frac{3}{4}$ with $\frac{6}{8}$ so that the denominators are the same.

$= \frac{7}{8}$

- Add the numerators: $1 + 6 = 7$. **Do not add** the denominators; the denominator stays the same.

Example
$\frac{9}{12} - \frac{1}{3}$

- First make the denominators the same: $\frac{1}{3} \xrightarrow{\times 4} \frac{4}{12}$

  $\frac{1}{3}$ is equivalent to $\frac{4}{12}$.

$= \frac{9}{12} - \frac{4}{12}$

- Replace $\frac{1}{3}$ with $\frac{4}{12}$.

$= \frac{5}{12}$

- Subtract the numerators but **not** the denominators; the denominator stays the same number.

On a calculator you would type in: `9 a%  12 − 1 a% 3 =`

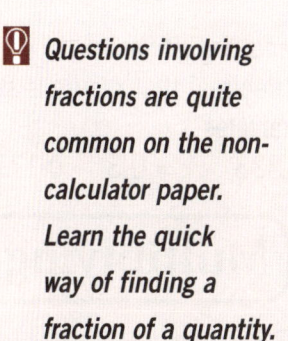

> Questions involving fractions are quite common on the non-calculator paper. Learn the quick way of finding a fraction of a quantity.

Proportional changes with fractions and percentages

Increase and decrease
There are two methods. Use the one that is familiar to you. Remember that 'of' means multiply.

Example
Last year there were 290 people belonging to a gym. This year there are $\frac{3}{5}$ more. How many people now belong?

Method 1
$\frac{3}{5} \times 290 = 174$
$290 + 174 = 464$ people

Work out $\frac{3}{5}$ **of** 290. Add this on to the original number.

Method 2
Increasing by $\frac{3}{5}$ is the same as multiplying by $1\frac{3}{5}$ ($1 + \frac{3}{5}$).
$1\frac{3}{5} \times 290 = 464$

On the calculator key in `1 a% 3 a% 5 × 290 =`

> Use the fraction key to work this out, if possible. If this question is on the non-calculator paper, remember to:
> - Divide 290 by the denominator $290 \div 5 = 58$
> - Multiply by the numerator $58 \times 3 = 174$
> - Now add onto the original value

KEY TERMS

Make sure you understand these terms before moving on!
- numerator
- denominator
- proper fraction
- improper fraction

QUICK TEST

1. Without using a calculator, work out the following:
   a) $\frac{2}{9} + \frac{3}{27}$
   b) $\frac{3}{5} - \frac{1}{4}$
   c) $\frac{6}{9} \times \frac{72}{104}$
   d) $\frac{8}{9} \div \frac{2}{3}$
   e) $\frac{4}{7} - \frac{1}{3}$
   f) $\frac{2}{7} \div 1\frac{1}{2}$
   g) $\frac{7}{11} \div \frac{22}{14}$
   h) $\frac{2}{9} + \frac{4}{7}$

2. Calculate $\frac{2}{9}$ of £180.

3. The rainfall this year was $\frac{7}{12}$ more than last year. If 156 mm fell last year, how much fell this year?

Decimals

A *decimal point* is used to separate whole number columns from fractional columns.

Example

Thousands	Hundreds	Tens	Units	.	Tenths	Hundredths	Thousandths
5	9	2	4	.	1	6	3

↑ Decimal point

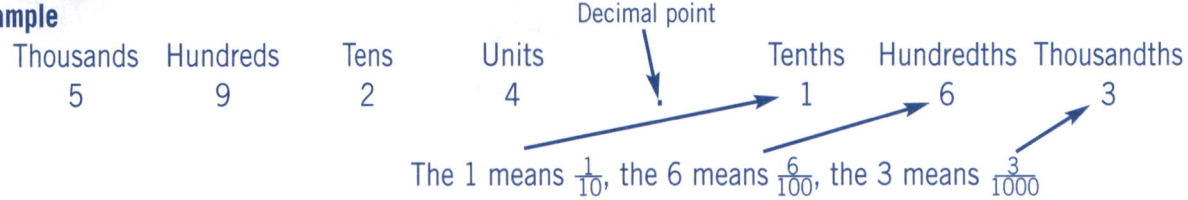

The 1 means $\frac{1}{10}$, the 6 means $\frac{6}{100}$, the 3 means $\frac{3}{1000}$

Recurring decimals

A decimal that recurs is shown by placing a dot over the numbers that repeat.

Examples

$0.333\ldots = 0.\dot{3}$ $0.17777\ldots = 0.1\dot{7}$ $0.232323\ldots = 0.\dot{2}\dot{3}$

Multiplying and dividing decimals by 10, 100, 1000

To multiply a **decimal** number by 10, 100, 1000, etc., move each digit one, two, three, etc. places to the left.

Examples

1. $8.7 \times 10 = 87$

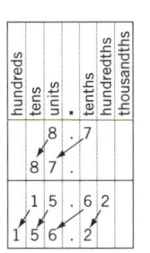

2. $15.62 \times 10 = 156.2$

You can use a similar method when multiplying decimal numbers by 100 or 1000.
$15.27 \times 100 = 1527$ $29.369 \times 1000 = 29369$

To divide decimals by 10, 100, 1000, etc., move each digit one, two, three, etc. places to the right.

Example

$146.2 \div 100 = 1.462$

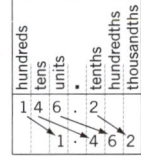

Ordering decimals

When ordering decimals:
- First write them with the same number of figures after the decimal point.
- Then compare whole numbers, digits in the tenths place, digits in the hundredths place, and so on.

💡 *Remember, hundredths are smaller than tenths:* $\frac{10}{100} = \frac{1}{10}$ so $\frac{6}{100} < \frac{1}{10}$

Examples

Arrange these numbers in order of size, smallest first:

6.21, 6.023, 6.4, 6.04, 2.71, 9.4
- First rewrite them:

6.210, 6.023, 6.400, 6.040, 2.710, 9.400
- Then re-order them:

2.710, 6.023, 6.040, 6.210, 6.400, 9.400

Multiplying and dividing by numbers between 0 and 1

When **multiplying** by numbers between 0 and 1, the result is always **smaller** than the starting value.
When **dividing** by numbers between 0 and 1, the result is always **bigger** than the starting value.

Examples

$6 \times 0.1 = 0.6$
$6 \times 0.01 = 0.06$
$6 \times 0.001 = 0.006$
The result is smaller than the starting value.

$6 \div 0.1 = 60$
$6 \div 0.01 = 600$
$6 \div 0.001 = 6000$
The result is bigger than the starting value.

Calculations with decimals

When **adding** and **subtracting** decimals, the decimal points need to go under each other.

Examples

```
  27.46
   7.291 +
  34.751
   1 1
```
Line up the digits carefully.

Put the decimal points under each other.

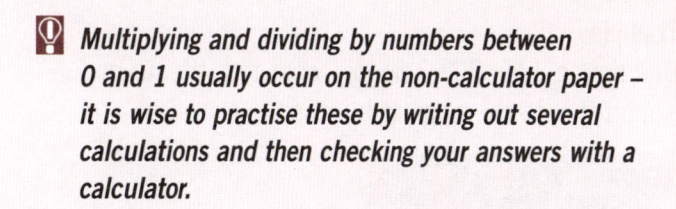

```
   6 9 1
  17.00
  12.84 −
   4.16
```
The decimal point in the answer will be in line.

When **multiplying** decimals, the answer must have the same number of decimal places as the total number of decimal places in the numbers which are being multiplied.

Examples

Work out 24.6 × 7

```
   246
     7 ×
  1722
   3 4
```
Multiply 246 by 7 = 1722, ignoring the decimal point. 24.6 has 1 number after the decimal point. The answer must have 1 decimal place (1 d.p.).

So 24.6 × 7 = 172.2

Work out 4.52 × 0.2

```
  452
    2 ×
  904
    1
```
Work out 452 × 2, ignoring the decimal points.
4.52 has 2 d.p.; 0.2 has 1 d.p.
So the answer must have 3 d.p.

904 → 0.904   Move the digits 3 places to the right.

So 4.52 × 0.2 = 0.904

When **dividing** decimals, divide as normal, placing the decimal points in line.

Example

```
     4.8
  3)14.²4
```
Put the decimal points in line.

> *Remember to check your answer with a calculator.*

> *Multiplying and dividing by numbers between 0 and 1 usually occur on the non-calculator paper – it is wise to practise these by writing out several calculations and then checking your answers with a calculator.*

KEY TERMS

Make sure you understand these terms before moving on!
- decimal point
- decimal
- recurring decimal

QUICK TEST

1 Without using a calculator, work out the following:
a) 27.16 + 9.32   b) 29.04 − 11.361   c) 12.8 × 2.1
d) 49.2 ÷ 4   e) 600 × 0.01   f) 520 × 0.1
g) 20 × 0.02   h) 37 × 0.0001   i) 400 ÷ 0.1
j) 450 ÷ 0.01   k) 470 ÷ 0.001   l) 650 ÷ 0.02

2 Arrange these numbers in order of size, smallest first.
a) 2.61, 4.02, 4.20, 4.021, 2.615, 2.607
b) 8.27, 8.206, 8.271, 6.49, 6.05, 8.93

3 Without using a calculator, work out the following.
a) 6.93 × 100   b) 29.1 × 10   c) 707.4 ÷ 100
d) 28.4 ÷ 1000   e) 7.65 × 1000   f) 27.19 ÷ 100

DECIMALS Number

Rounding

Rounding to the nearest 10, 100, 1000

Large numbers are often rounded to the nearest ten, hundred or thousand to make them easier to work with.

Rounding to the nearest ten
Look at the **digit** in the units column. If it is less than 5, round down. If it is 5 or more, round up.

Example
276 people went to the theatre to see the opening night of a play.
Round this to the nearest ten.

There is a 6 in the units column.
6 > 5, so round up to 280.
276 is 280 to the nearest ten.

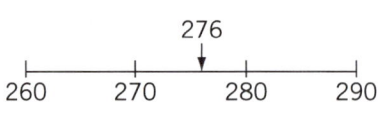

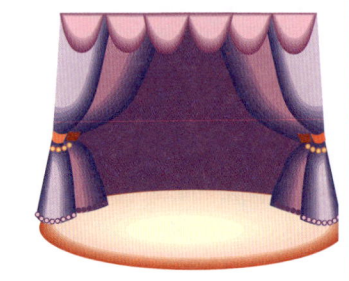

Rounding to the nearest hundred
Look at the digit in the tens column. If it is less than 5, round down. If it is 5 or more, round up.

Example
One day in July, 3250 people went to a theme park.
Round this to the nearest hundred.

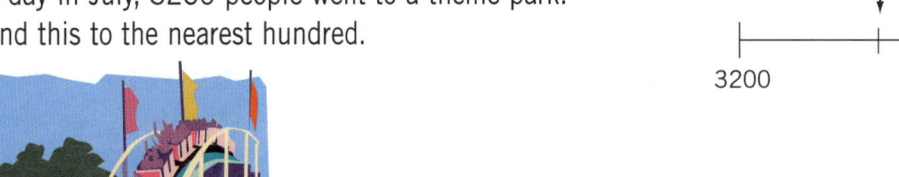

Since there is a 5 in the tens column, you round up to 3300.
3250 is 3300 to the nearest hundred.

Rounding to the nearest thousand
Look at the digits in the hundreds column.
The same rules apply as for rounding to the nearest 10 or 100.

Example
17 436 people attended a football match.
Round 17 436 to the nearest thousand.
There is a 4 in the hundreds column, so round down to 17 000.
17 436 is 17 000 to the nearest thousand.

Similar methods can be used to round any number to any power of 10.
Rounded numbers are often used in newspaper reports.

Decimal places (d.p.)

When rounding numbers to a specified number of **decimal places**:
- Look at the last number that is wanted (e.g. if rounding 12.367 to 2 d.p., look at the 6 which is the second d.p.).
- Look at the number to the right of it (the number which is not needed – in this case, the 7).
- If it is **5 or more**, then **round up** the last digit (7 is greater than 5, so round up the 6 to a 7).
- If it is **less than 5**, then the last digit remains the **same**.

Examples
Round 12.49 to 1 d.p.
12.4**9** rounds up to 12.5.

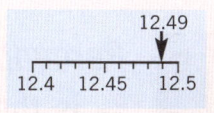

Round 8.735 to 2 d.p.
8.73**5** rounds up to 8.74.

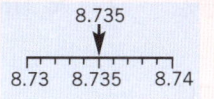

Round 9.624 to 2 d.p.
9.62**4** rounds down to 9.62.

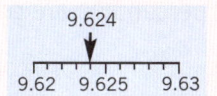

Significant figures (s.f. or sig. fig.)

The first **significant figure** is the first digit which is not zero. The 2nd, 3rd, 4th, ... significant figures follow on after the first digit. They may or may not be zeros.

Examples

6 . 4 0 2 7 has 5 s.f.
1st 2nd 3rd 4th 5th

0 . 0 0 0 4 7 0 1 has 4 s.f.
1st 2nd 3rd 4th

To round to a given number of significant figures, apply the same rule as with decimal places: if the next digit is 5 or more, round up.

Examples

Number	to 3 s.f.	to 2 s.f.	to 1 s.f.
4.207	4.21	4.2	4
4379	4380	4400	4000
0.006209	0.00621	0.0062	0.006

Take care when rounding that you do not change the place values.

After rounding the last digit, you must fill in the end zeros.
For example, 4380 = 4400 to 2 s.f. (not 44).

KEY TERMS

Make sure you understand these terms before moving on!
- digit
- decimal place
- significant figure

QUICK TEST

1. Round the following numbers to the nearest 10.
   a) 26   b) 2735   c) 1052   d) 32769

2. Round the following numbers to 2 decimal places.
   a) 6.429   b) 18.607   c) 14.271   d) 29.638

3. Round the following numbers to 2 significant figures.
   a) 2768   b) 271   c) 38946   d) 0.0273

Percentages 1

75% *Percentages* are fractions with a denominator of 100.
% is the percentage sign.
75% means $\frac{75}{100}$ (this is also equal to $\frac{3}{4}$).

Example
A mixed bag of nuts contains 26% cashew nuts, 42% peanuts and the rest are pistachio nuts. What percentage are pistachio nuts?

$$26 + 42 = 68\% \text{ other nuts}$$
Percentage of pistachio nuts $= 100 - 68$
$= 32\%$

Percentage of a quantity

The word '**of**' means **multiply**. For example,
40% of £600 becomes $\frac{40}{100} \times 600 = £240$
On the calculator, key in
`40 ÷ 100 × 600 =`
If this is on the non-calculator paper
- Work out 10% first by dividing by 10
  e.g. $600 \div 10 = £60$
- Multiply by 4 to get 40%, i.e. $4 \times 60 = £240$

Examples
Find 15% of £750, without using a calculator.

$10\% = \frac{1}{10}$ so 10% of £750 $= \frac{750}{10} = £75$

5% is half of 75 = £37.50

So 15% = 75 + 37.50
= £112.50

Find 17.5% of £640, without using a calculator.
10%	$= 640 \div 10 = £64$
5%	$= £32$
2.5%	$= £16$
So 17.5%	$= 64 + 32 + 16$
	$= £112$

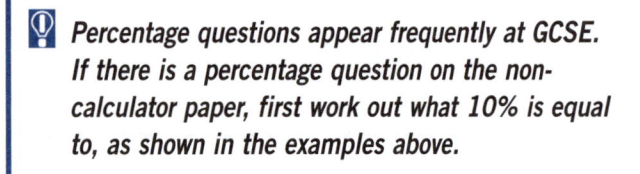

💡 *Percentage questions appear frequently at GCSE. If there is a percentage question on the non-calculator paper, first work out what 10% is equal to, as shown in the examples above.*

Example
A meal for four costs £92.20. VAT (value added tax) is charged at 17.5%.
- VAT is a tax which is added on to the cost of most items.

a) How much VAT is there to pay on the meal?
b) What is the final price of the meal?

a) 17.5% of £92.20 $= \frac{17.5}{100} \times 92.20$
$= £16.14$ (to the nearest penny)
VAT = £16.14

This is just like a percentage of quantity question.

b) Price of meal = £92.20 + £16.14 = £108.34

An alternative is to use a scale factor method:
- An increase of 17.5%, is the same as multiplying by $1 + \frac{17.5}{100} = 1.175$.

£92.20 × 1.175 = £108.34 (to the nearest penny)

One quantity as a percentage of another

To find one quantity as a percentage of another, form a fraction and **multiply by 100%**.

fraction $\xrightarrow{\times 100\%}$ percentage

Example
In a carton of milk, 6.2g of the contents are fat. If 2.5g of the fat is saturated, what percentage of the total fat content is this?

$\frac{2.5}{6.2} \times 100\% = 40.3\%$ (to 1 d.p.)

On the calculator, key in
2.5 ÷ 6.2 × 100 =

Percentage increase and decrease

Since we know the answer to a percentage increase and decrease will be a percentage, we must multiply by 100%.

$$\% \text{ change} = \frac{\text{change}}{\text{original}} \times 100\%$$

Example
A coat costs £125. In a sale the price is reduced to £85.
What is the percentage reduction?
Reduction = £125 − £85 = £40
Reduction = $\frac{40}{125} \times 100\%$
= 32%

Example
Matthew bought a flat for £45 000.
Three years later, he sold it for £62 000.
What was his percentage profit?

Profit = £62 000 − £45 000
= £17 000

% Profit = $\frac{17000}{45000} \times 100\%$
= 37.78%

KEY TERMS

Make sure you understand this term before moving on!
- percentage

QUICK TEST

1. Work out 30% of £700.
2. Sarah got 94 out of 126 in a Maths test. What percentage did she get? **C**
3. Reece weighed 6 lb when he was born. If his weight has increased by 65%, how much does he now weigh? **C**
4. Super's football boots — $\frac{1}{3}$ off   Joe's football boots — 28% off **C**

   If a pair of football boots usually costs £49.99, which shop sells them cheaper in the sale and what is the sale price?

C *Indicates that a calculator may be used.*

Percentages 2

Repeated percentage change

Example
A car was bought for £8000 in 2004. Each year it depreciated in value by 20%.
What is the car worth 3 years later?

Method 1
- First find 80% of the value of the car.

    Year 1 $\frac{80}{100}$ × £8000 = £6400

Work these questions out year by year.

Beware: do not do 3 × 20 = 60% reduction over 3 years!

- Then work out the value year by year.

    Year 2 $\frac{80}{100}$ × £6400 = £5120 (£6400 depreciated in value by 20%)

    Year 3 $\frac{80}{100}$ × £5120 = £4096 after 3 years (£5120 depreciated by 20%)

Method 2
A quick way to work this out uses the **scale factor** method.
- Finding 80% of the value of the car is the same as multiplying by 0.8. The **scale factor** is 0.8.

    Year 1   0.8 × £8000 = £6400
    Year 2   0.8 × £6400 = £5120
    Year 3   0.8 × £5120 = £4096

This is the same as working out $(0.8)^3$ × 8000 = £4096
A much quicker way if you understand it; and also useful to know in everyday life.

Simple interest

This is the interest that is sometimes paid on money in banks and building societies. The interest is paid each year (**per annum** or **p.a.**) and is the same amount each year.

Example
Jonathan has £2500 in his savings account. **Simple interest** is paid at 4.4% p.a. How much does he have in his account at the end of the year?
(This is a 'percentage of' question.)

100 + 4.4 = 104.4% (increasing by 4.4% is the same as multiplying by 100 + 4.4 = 104.4%)

Total savings = $\frac{104.4}{100}$ × £2500 = £2610

Interest paid = £2610 − £2500 = £110

Note: If the money was in the account for 4 years, the interest at the end of the 4 years would be 4 × £110 = £440.

Compound interest

This is the type of interest where the bank pays interest on the interest earned as well as on the original money.

Example
If Jonathan has £2500 in his savings account and **compound interest** is paid at 4.4% p.a., how much will he have in his account after 2 years?

Method 1
Year 1: $\frac{104.4}{100}$ × £2500 = £2610
Year 2: 1.044 × £2610 = £2724.84
Total after 2 years = £2724.84

Method 2
Using the scale factor method:
$\frac{104.4}{100}$ = 1.044 is the scale factor

£2500 × 1.044 × 1.044
= 2500 × $(1.044)^2$
Total after 2 years = £2724.84

Tax and National Insurance

National Insurance
National Insurance (NI) is usually deducted as a percentage from a wage.

Example
Sue earns £1402.65 a month. National Insurance at 9% is deducted. How much NI must she pay?

9% of £1402.65 = 0.09 × £1402.65 = £126.24

Income Tax
A percentage of a wage or salary is removed as **income tax**.
Personal allowances must first be deducted in order to obtain the **taxable income**.

Example
Harold earns £190 per week. The first £62 is not taxable but the remainder is taxed at 24%. How much income tax does he pay each week?

Taxable income = £190 − £62 = £128
24% tax   = 0.24 × £128 = £30.72
Tax per week   = £30.72

> Being able to answer questions like the examples shown in this section is important – not only because they appear on the examination paper but because you will come across them in everyday life. Most of the examples are 'percentage of' questions.
>
> There are really only 2 types of percentage questions:
> 1. 'Percentage of'. Here you are given the percentage so you divide by 100.
> 2. Writing your answer as a percentage. Here you need to work out a percentage so you multiply by 100.

KEY TERMS
Make sure you understand these terms before moving on!
- simple interest
- compound interest
- National Insurance
- income tax

QUICK TEST

1. Charlotte has £4250 in the bank. If the interest rate is 6.8% p.a., how much interest on the savings will she get at the end of one year? (C)

2. A car costs £6000 cash or can be bought by hire purchase with a 30% deposit followed by 12 monthly instalments of £365. Find: (C)
   a) the deposit
   b) the total amount paid for the car if bought by hire purchase.

3. A flat was bought in 1998 for £62000. In 1999 the price increased by 20% and then by a further 35% in 2000. How much was the flat worth at the end of 2000? (C)

4. Fiona has £3200 savings. If compound interest is paid at 3% p.a., how much will she have in her account after 2 years? (C)

(C) *Indicates that a calculator may be used.*

Equivalents

Fractions to decimals to percentages

Fractions, decimals and percentages all mean the same thing but are just written in different ways.

Fraction	Decimal	Percentage
$\frac{1}{2}$	0.5	50%
$\frac{1}{3}$	0.3̇3̇	33.3̇%
$\frac{2}{3}$	0.6̇6̇	66.6̇%
$\frac{1}{4}$	0.25	25%
$\frac{3}{4}$	0.75	75%
$\frac{1}{5}$	0.2	20%
$\frac{1}{8}$	0.125	12.5%
$\frac{3}{8}$	0.375	37.5%
$\frac{1}{10}$	0.1	10%
$\frac{1}{100}$	0.01	1%

For $\frac{3}{4}$: $3 \div 4 \rightarrow 0.75 \xrightarrow{\times 100\%} 75\%$

The above table shows
- Some common fractions and their equivalents which you need to learn.
- How to convert fractions to decimals to percentages.

Ordering different types of numbers

When putting fractions, decimals and percentages in order of size, it is best to change them all to decimals first.

Example
Place the following in order of size, smallest first.
$\frac{3}{5}$, 0.65, 0.273, 27%, 62%, $\frac{4}{9}$

0.6, 0.65, 0.273, 0.27, 0.62, 0.4̇4̇   Convert fractions and percentages into decimals first.

0.27, 0.273, 0.4̇4̇, 0.6, 0.62, 0.65   Now order.

💡 *Get a friend to test you on the equivalences between fractions, decimals and percentages as you need to know them.*

QUICK TEST

1. Change the following fractions into
   a) decimals   b) percentages (C)
   i) $\frac{2}{7}$ ii) $\frac{3}{5}$ iii) $\frac{8}{9}$

2. Place the following in order of size, smallest first.
   $\frac{2}{5}$, 0.42, 0.041, $\frac{1}{3}$, 5%, 26%

   (C) Indicates that a calculator may be used.

Using a calculator

Order of operations

BIDMAS is a made-up word which helps you to remember the order in which calculations take place.

$$B \quad I \quad D \quad M \quad A \quad S$$

Brackets Indices or powers Division Multiplication Addition Subtraction

This means that brackets are worked out first, followed by indices, multiplication and division, then addition and subtraction.

Examples

$(5 + 2) \times 3 = 21$
Do the calculation in brackets first:
$5 + 2 = 7$ then $7 \times 3 = 21$.

$5 + 2 \times 3 = 11$
Here there are no brackets, so the multiplication is carried out first, then $5 + 6 = 11$.

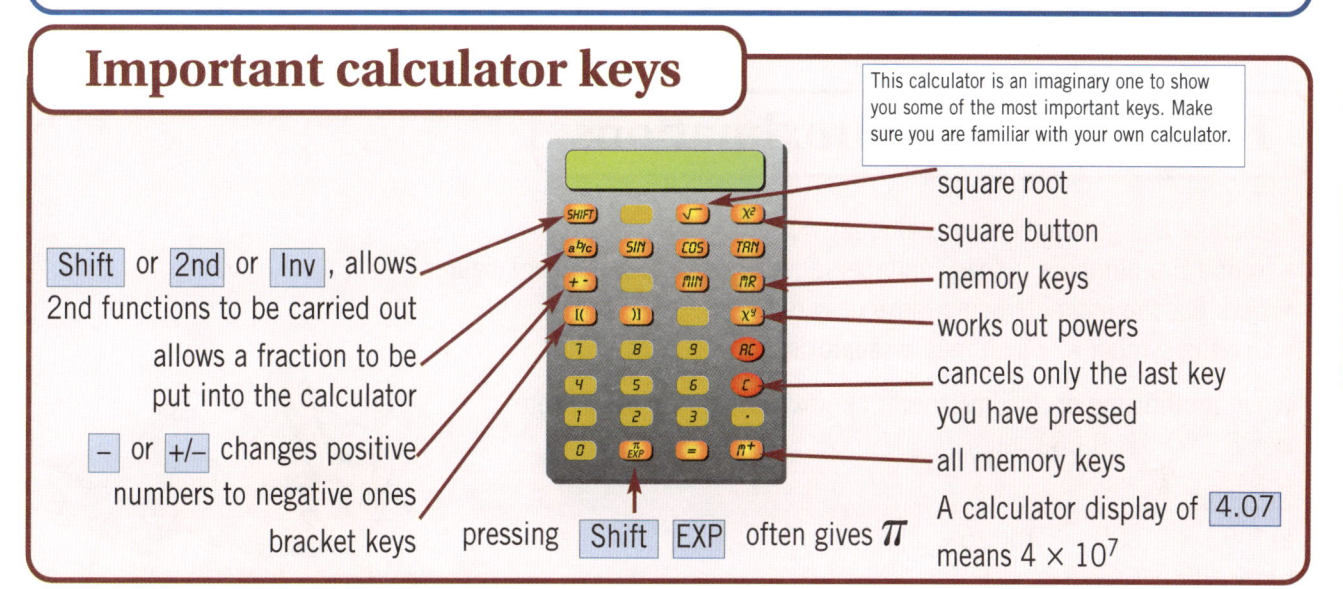

Important calculator keys

This calculator is an imaginary one to show you some of the most important keys. Make sure you are familiar with your own calculator.

- square root
- square button
- memory keys
- works out powers
- cancels only the last key you have pressed
- all memory keys
- A calculator display of 4.07 means 4×10^7

- Shift or 2nd or Inv, allows 2nd functions to be carried out
- allows a fraction to be put into the calculator
- − or +/− changes positive numbers to negative ones
- bracket keys
- pressing Shift EXP often gives π

Calculating powers

y^x or x^y is used for calculating powers, e.g. 2^7.
- Use the power key on the calculator to work out 2^7.
- Write down calculator keys used.
- Check that you obtain the answer 128.

Now try writing down the keys that would be needed for these calculations.
Check that you get the right answers.

a) $\frac{2.9 \times 3.6}{(4.2 + 3.7)} = 1.322$ b) $9^2 \times 4^5 = 82944$ c) $\frac{3 \times (5.2)^2}{9.6 \times (12.4)^3} = 4.432 \times 10^{-3}$

> Make sure you know how to use the power key. It can save lots of time.

QUICK TEST

1. Work out these on your calculator:

   a) $\frac{27.1 \times 6.4}{9.3 + 2.7}$ b) $\frac{(9.3)^4}{2.7 \times 3.6}$

   c) $\sqrt{\frac{25^2}{4\pi}}$ d) $\frac{5}{9}(25 - 10)$

Approximating & checking calculations

Checking calculations

When checking calculations, the process can be reversed like this:

Examples

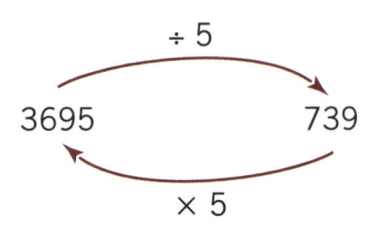

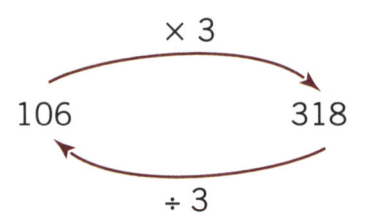

3695 ÷ 5 → 739 (÷ 5)
739 × 5 → 3695 (× 5)

3695 ÷ 5 = 739
Check: 739 × 5 = 3695

106 × 3 → 318 (× 3)
318 ÷ 3 → 106 (÷ 3)

106 × 3 = 318
Check: 318 ÷ 3 = 106

Estimates and approximations

Estimating is a good way of checking answers.
- Round the numbers to 'easy' numbers, usually 1 or 2 significant figures.
- Work out the estimate using these easy numbers.
- Use the symbol ≈, which means '**approximately equal to**'.

When multiplying or dividing, never approximate a number to zero.
Use 0.1, 0.01, 0.001, etc.

Examples
a) $8.93 \times 25.09 \approx 10 \times 25 = 250$
b) $(6.29)^2 \approx 6^2 = 36$
c) $\frac{296 \times 52.1}{9.72 \times 1.14} \approx \frac{300 \times 50}{10 \times 1} = \frac{15000}{10} = 1500$
d) $0.096 \times 79.2 \approx 0.1 \times 80 = 8$

Example
Jack does the calculation $\frac{9.6 \times 103}{(2.9)^2}$
a) Estimate the answer to this calculation, without using a calculator.
b) Jack's answer is 1175.7. Is this the **right order of magnitude** (about the right size)?

a) Estimate: $\frac{9.6 \times 103}{(2.9)^2} \approx \frac{10 \times 100}{3^2} = \frac{1000}{9} \approx \frac{1000}{10} = 100$

b) Jack's answer is not the right order of magnitude. It is 10 times too big.

When adding and subtracting, very small numbers may be approximated to zero.

Examples
$109.6 + 0.0002 \approx 110 + 0 = 110$ $63.87 - 0.01 \approx 64 - 0 = 64$

💡 Questions which involve approximating are common on the non-calculator paper. For most of these questions, you are expected to round to 1 significant figure. Even if you find the calculation difficult, show your approximations to pick up method marks.

Calculations

When solving problems, the answers should be rounded sensibly.

Example
95.26 × 6.39 = 608.7114 = 608.71 (2 d.p.)
(Round to 2 d.p. because the values in the question are to 2 d.p.)

Example
Jackie has £9.37. She divides it as equally as she can between 5 people. How much does each person receive?
£9.37 ÷ 5 = £1.874
 = £1.87
(Round to 1.87 as it is money.)

Example
Paint is sold in 8 litre tins. Sandra needs 27 litres of paint. How many tins must she buy?
27 ÷ 8 = 3 remainder 3
Sandra needs 4 tins of paint.
Sandra would not have enough paint with 3 tins – she would be 3 litres short. Hence the number of tins of paint must be rounded up.

> You will lose marks if you do not write money to 2 d.p. If the answer to a money calculation is £9.7, always write it to 2 d.p. as £9.70.

Example
The price of a basic calculator is £2.30. Mr Baur wants to buy some basic calculators. He has £70 to spend. Work out the greatest number of basic calculators he can buy.

70 ÷ 2.30 = 30.434... calculators

The greatest number of basic calculators that Mr Baur can buy is 30.

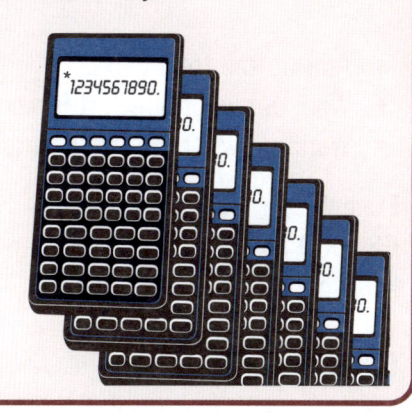

> When rounding remainders, consider the context of the question.

KEY TERMS

Make sure you understand this term before moving on!
- estimating

QUICK TEST

1. Estimate the answer to $\frac{(29.4)^2 + 106}{2.2 \times 5.1}$

2. Sukvinder decided to decorate her living room. The total area of the walls was 48 m². If one roll of wallpaper covers 5 m² of wall, how many rolls of wallpaper did Sukvinder need?

3. Thomas earned £109.25 for working a 23-hour week. How much was he paid per hour?
Check your calculation by estimating. **C**

C *Indicates that a calculator may be used.*

APPROXIMATING & CHECKING CALCULATIONS

Number

Ratio

Ratios

- A **ratio** is used to compare two or more related quantities.
- '**Compared to**' is replaced with **two dots** (**:**) For example, '16 boys compared to 20 girls' can be written as 16 : 20.
- To simplify ratios, divide both parts of the ratio by their highest common factor. For example,
  16 : 20 = 4 : 5
  (Divide both sides by 4.)

When ratios are simplified as much as they can be, they are in their **simplest form**.

Examples
- Simplify the ratio 21 : 28.
  21 : 28 = 3 : 4 (Divide both sides by 7).
- The ratio of maroon flowers to blue flowers can be written:
  10 : 4
  = $\frac{10}{2} : \frac{4}{2}$
  = 5 : 2

In other words, for every 5 maroon flowers there are 2 blue flowers.
To express the ratio 5 : 2 in the ratio n : 1, divide both sides by 2.
5 : 2 = $\frac{5}{2} : \frac{2}{2}$
= 2.5 : 1

Sharing a quantity in a given ratio

- Add up the total parts.
- Work out what one part is worth.
- Work out what the other parts are worth.

Example
£20 000 is shared between Ewan and Leroy in the ratio 1 : 4. How much does each receive?
1 + 4 = 5 parts
5 parts = £20 000
1 part = $\frac{£20\,000}{5}$ = £4000
So Ewan gets 1 × £4000 = £4000 and Leroy gets 4 × £4000 = £16 000.

Best buys

Compare **unit amounts** to decide which option is the better value for money.

Example
The same brand of coffee is sold in two different sized jars.
Which jar represents the better value for money?
- Find the cost per gram for both jars.
  The 100 g jar costs 186p, so 186 ÷ 100 = 1.86p per gram.
  The 250 g jar costs 247p, so 247 ÷ 250 = 0.988p per gram.
- Since the larger jar costs less per gram it gives the better value for money.

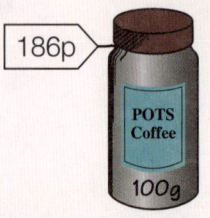

Increasing and decreasing in a given ratio

- Divide to get one part.
- Multiply for each new part.

Example
A photograph of length 9 cm is to be enlarged in the ratio 5 : 3.
What is the length of the enlarged photograph?
- First divide 9 cm by 3 to get 1 part:
  $9 \div 3 = 3$
- Multiply this by 5. So 9 cm becomes $5 \times 3 = 15$ cm on the enlarged photograph.

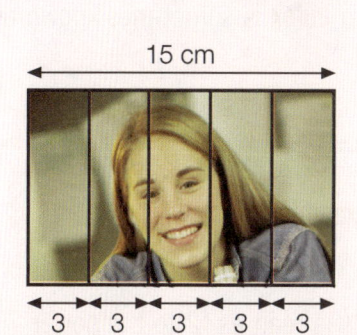

Example
A house took 8 people 6 days to build.
At the same rate, how long would it take 3 people?

Time for 8 people = 6 days
Time for 1 person = $8 \times 6 = 48$ days
(It takes 1 person longer to build the house.)
3 people will take $\frac{1}{3}$ of the time taken by 1 person.
Time for 3 people = $\frac{48}{3} = 16$ days.

Example
A recipe for 4 people needs 1600 g of flour.
How much flour is needed for 6 people?
- Divide 1600 g by 4, so 400 g for 1 person.
- Multiply by 6, so $6 \times 400\text{g} = 2400\text{g}$ flour is needed for 6 people.

> **When answering problems of the type shown here always try and work out what a unit (or one) is worth. You should then be able to work out what any other value is worth.**

KEY TERMS

Make sure you understand this term before moving on!
- ratio

QUICK TEST

1. Write the following ratios in their simplest form:
   a) 12 : 15
   b) 6 : 12
   c) 25 : 10

2. Three sisters share 60 sweets between them in the ratios 2 : 3 : 7. How many sweets does each sister receive?

3. If 15 oranges cost £1.80, how much will 23 identical oranges cost? **(C)**

4. A map is being enlarged in the ratio 12 : 7. If the road length was 21 cm on the original map, what is the length of the road on the enlarged map? **(C)**

(C) *Indicates that a calculator may be used.*

Indices

Indices

An **index** is sometimes known as a **power**.

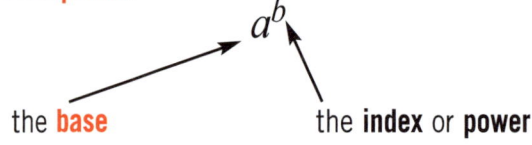

$$a^b$$

the **base** → a ; the **index** or **power** → b

Examples

6^4 is read as '6 to the power of 4'. It means $6 \times 6 \times 6 \times 6$.

2^7 is read as '2 to the power 7'. It means $2 \times 2 \times 2 \times 2 \times 2 \times 2 \times 2$.

- The base has to be the same when the rules of indices are applied.

Rules of indices

You need to learn these rules as indices are a very common topic in the non-calculator paper:

- When **multiplying**, **add** the powers.

  $4^7 \times 4^3 = 4^{7+3} = 4^{10}$

- When **dividing**, **subtract** the powers.

  $6^9 \div 6^4 = 6^{9-4} = 6^5$

- Anything raised to the **power 0** is just **1**, provided the number is not 0.

  $5^0 = 1$ $6^0 = 1$

  $2.7189^0 = 1$ $0^0 =$ undefined

- Anything to the **power 1** is just **itself**.

  $15^1 = 15$ $1923^1 = 1923$

The above rules also apply when the powers are negative.

Examples

$6^{-2} \times 6^{12} = 6^{-2+12} = 6^{10}$

$5^6 \div 5^4 = 5^{6-4} = 5^2$

$8^4 \times 8^{-3} = 8^{4+-3} = 8^1 = 8$

$4^3 \times 4^{10} = 4^{3+10} = 4^{13}$

$7^{10} \div 7^4 = 7^{10-4} = 7^6$

Indices and algebra

The rules that apply with numbers also apply with letters.

Laws of indices

$a^n \times a^m = a^{n+m}$

$a^n \div a^m = a^{n-m}$

$a^1 = a$

Examples

$x^4 \times x^7 = x^{11}$ — Note that the numbers are multiplied

$a^{10} \div a^4 = a^6$

$4x^2 \times 3x^5 = 12x^7$ — but the powers of the same letter are added

$12x^5 \div 2x^2 = 6x^3$

$a^4 \times 3a^5 = 3a^9$

Simplify $\dfrac{3x^7 \times 4x^9}{6x^4}$

$\dfrac{3x^7 \times 4x^9}{6x^4} = \dfrac{12x^{16}}{6x^4} = 2x^{12}$

Work this out in 2 stages

Simplify $x^6 \times 4x^3$
$x^6 \times 4x^3 = 4x^9$

Simplify $\dfrac{12a^2b^3}{6a^3b^2}$

$\dfrac{12a^2b^3}{6a^3b^2} = \dfrac{2b}{a}$

Simplify $\dfrac{4a^4b^3}{2ab}$

$\dfrac{4a^4b^3}{2ab} = 2a^3b^2$

💡 *Indices questions are a very common topic on the non-calculator paper – learn the rules and you should be OK!*

KEY TERMS

Make sure you understand these terms before moving on!
- index
- power
- base

QUICK TEST

1. Simplify the following:
   a) $12^4 \times 12^8$ b) $9^2 \times 9^4$ c) 4^1
   d) $18^6 \div 18^{-2}$ e) $4^7 \times 4^{-2}$ f) 1^{20}

2. Simplify the following:
   a) $x^4 \times x^9$ b) $2x^9 \times 3x^7$ c) $12x^4 \div 3x^2$
   d) $25x^9 \div 5x^{-2}$ e) $\dfrac{5x^6 \times 4x^9}{10x^3}$

Practice questions

Use these questions to test your progress.
Check your answers on page 92.

1. From this list of numbers (2, 9, 21, 40, 41, 64, 100):
   a) Write down the numbers that are odd ....
   b) Write down the square numbers ....
   c) Write down the prime numbers ....
   d) Write down any numbers which are factors of 80 ....
   e) Write down any numbers which are multiples of 4 ....

2. The temperature outside is −6°, inside it is 15° higher.
   What is the temperature inside? ....

3. Work out the answers to:
   a) 589×76 b) $1674 \div 62$

   ....

4. Write these numbers in figures.
   a) fifty-six b) five hundred and eight c) seven thousand and two

   ....

5. Write the number 6 457 279 in words.

   ....

6. Put these numbers in order of size, smallest to largest.
   639   728   405   736   829   27

   ....

7. Mohammed needs some tiles for the kitchen floor. The tiles are sold in boxes of 8. Mohammed works out that he needs 60 tiles. How many boxes will he need to buy?

   ....

8. Hussain scored 58 marks out of 75 in a test. What percentage did he get?   (C)

   ....

9. A school raises £525 at the summer fair. 60% of the money raised is used to repair the tennis courts. How much is used to repair the tennis courts?

   ....

10. Arrange these decimals in order of size, smallest to largest.
    6.39   5.42   5.04   6.27   6.385   5.032

    ....

11. Write the ratio 12 : 15 in its simplest form.

    ....

12. The ingredients for 8 small cakes are:
    - 300 g self-raising flour
    - 150 g butter
    - 250 g sugar
    - 2 eggs

    Andrew is making 20 small cakes. Write down the amount he will need of each ingredient.
    .... g self-raising flour
    .... g butter
    .... g sugar
    .... eggs

(C) *Indicates that a calculator may be used.*

13. Mrs Jones inherits £55 000. She divides the money between her children in the ratio 3 : 3 : 5. How much does the child with the largest share receive?

   ....

14. Work these out on your calculator, giving your answers to 3 s.f.

   a) $\dfrac{4.2\,(3.6 + 5.1)}{2 - 1.9} =$ b) $\dfrac{3.8 + 4.6}{2.9 \times 4.1} =$ (C)

   ....

15. Show how you would estimate the answer to this expression without using a calculator. Work out the estimate.

   $\dfrac{8.7 + 9.02}{0.2 \times 48}$

   ....

16. Toothpaste is sold in three different sized tubes.

   50 ml = £1.24   75 ml = £1.96   100 ml = £2.42   (C)

   Which of the tubes of toothpaste is the best value for money?
   You must show full working out in order to justify your answer.

   ....

17. A piece of writing paper is 0.01 cm thick. A notepad has 150 sheets of paper. How thick is the notepad?

   ....

18. A car was bought in 2004 for £9000. Each year it depreciates in value by 15%. What is the car worth two years later?   (C)

   ....

19. James put £632 in a new savings account. At the end of every year interest at 4.2% is added to the amount in his savings account at the beginning of that year. Calculate the amount in James's savings account at the end of 3 years.   (C)

   ....

20. The price of a television has risen from £350 to £420. Work out the percentage increase in the price.

   ....

21. Simplify the following:

   a) $2^3 \times 3^2$

   b) $a^4 \times a^3$

   c) $b^6 \div b^2$

   d) $\dfrac{2a^5 \times 8a^4}{4a^2}$

   ....

How well did you do?   ✗ 0–5 Try again   6–10 Getting there   11–16 Good work   17–21 Excellent! ✓

Algebra 1

Algebraic conventions

- A **term** is a collection of numbers, letters and/or brackets, all multiplied together.
- Terms are separated by + and − signs. Each term has a **+** or **−** attached to the front of it.
- An **expression** is a group of terms.

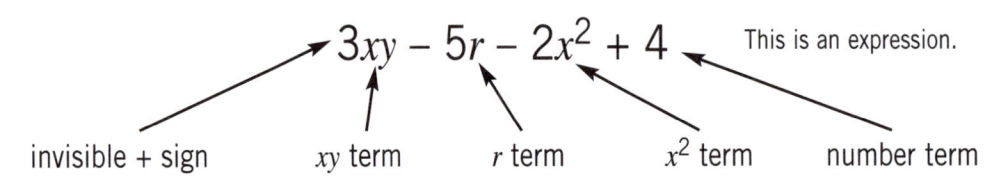

$$3xy - 5r - 2x^2 + 4$$

This is an expression.

invisible + sign → $3xy$ term, r term, x^2 term, number term

- $3 \times a$ is written without the multiplication sign as $3a$.

  $a + a + a = 3a$
  $a \times a \times a = a^3$, not $3a$

  $a \times a \times 2 = 2a^2$, not $(2a)^2$
  $a \times b \times 2 = 2ab$

Collecting like terms

Expressions can be simplified by collecting **like terms**.
Only collect the terms if their letters and powers are **identical**.

Examples

$4a + 2a = 6a$ Add the a terms together, then the terms with b. Remember that a means $1a$.

$3a^2 + 6a^2 - 4a^2 = 5a^2$

$4a + 6b - 3a + 2b = a + 8b$

$9a + 4b$ This cannot be simplified – there are no like terms.

$3xy + 2yx = 5xy$ Remember xy means the same as yx.

Writing formulae

Quite often in the exam you are given some information or a diagram and asked to write a formula based on it.

Example
Frances buys x books at £2.50 each. She pays with a £20 note. If she receives C pounds change, write down a formula for C.

$C = 20 - 2.50x$

This is the amount of money she spent.

Notice that no £ signs are put in the formula.

If in doubt, check by substituting a value for x, i.e.:
if she bought 1 book $x = 1$, so her change would be $20 - 2.50 \times 1 = £17.50$.

Example
Some patterns are made by using grey and white paving slabs.

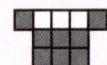

Write a formula for the number of grey paving slabs (g) in a pattern that uses (w) white slabs.

The formula is $g = 2w + 2$

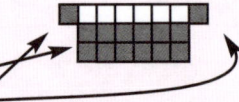

$2w$ represents the 2 layers; + 2 gives the grey slabs which are on either end of the white ones.

Formulae, expressions and substituting

$p + 3$ is an **expression**.
$y = p + 3$ is a **formula**. The value of y depends on the value of p.

Replacing a letter with a number is called **substitution**. When substituting:

- Write out the expression first and then replace the letters with the values given.
- Work out the value on your calculator. Use bracket keys where necessary and pay attention to the order of operations (BIDMAS).

Examples
Using $W = 5.6$, $t = -7.1$ and $u = \frac{2}{5}$, find the value of these expressions, giving your answers to 3 s.f.

a) $\frac{W+t}{u}$ b) $W - \frac{t}{u}$ c) $\sqrt{Wt^2}$

Remember to show the substitutions.

a) $\frac{W+t}{u} = \frac{5.6 + (-7.1)}{\frac{2}{5}} = -3.75$

b) $W - \frac{t}{u} = 5.6 - \frac{(-7.1)}{\frac{2}{5}} = 23.4$

c) $\sqrt{Wt^2} = \sqrt{5.6 \times (-7.1)^2} = 16.8$

> When substituting into an expression or formula you must show each step in your working out. By showing your substitution you will obtain method marks even if you get the final answer wrong.

You may need to treat t^2 as $(-7.1)^2$, depending on your calculator.

Using formulae

A formula describes the relationship between two (or more) variables.
A formula must have an = sign in it.

Example
Andrew hires a van. There is a standing charge of £8 and then it costs £3 per hour. How much does it cost for:

a) 6 hours' drive
b) y hours' drive
c) Write a formula for the total hire cost C.

a) $8 + (3 \times 6) = £26$
b) $8 + (3 \times y) = 8 + 3y$
c) $C = 8 + 3y$ This is a formula which works out the cost of hiring the van for any number of hours.

KEY TERMS

Make sure you understand these terms before moving on!

- term
- expression
- formula
- substitution

QUICK TEST

1. Simplify these expressions by collecting like terms:
   a) $5a + 2a + 3a$
   b) $6a - 3b + 4b + 2a$
   c) $5x - 3x + 7x - 2y + 6y$
   d) $3xy^2 - 2x^2y + 6x^2y - 8xy^2$

2. Using $p = 6.2$, $r = -3.2$ and $s = \frac{2}{3}$, find the value of these expressions, giving your answer to 3 s.f. Use a calculator. (C)
   a) $pr + s$ b) $p^2s - r$
   c) $r^2 - \frac{p}{s}$ d) $(ps - r)^2$

Algebra 2

Multiplying out brackets

- Multiplying out brackets helps to simplify algebraic expressions.
- The term outside the brackets multiplies each separate term inside the brackets.

Examples

$3(2x + 5) = 6x + 15$ $(3 \times 2x = 6x, 3 \times 5 = 15)$

$a(3a - 4) = 3a^2 - 4a$ $b(2a + 3b - c) = 2ab + 3b^2 - bc$

If the term outside the bracket is **negative**, all of the signs of the terms inside the bracket are **changed** when multiplying out.

Examples

$-4(2x + 3) = -8x - 12$ $-2(4 - 3x) = -8 + 6x$

To simplify expressions, expand the brackets first then collect like terms.

Example

Expand and simplify $2(x - 3) + 3(x + 4)$.

$2(x - 3) + 3(x + 4)$
$= 2x - 6 + 3x + 12$ Multiply out the brackets.
$= 5x + 6$ Collect like terms.

💡 If you are asked to '**expand**' brackets it just means multiply them out. When you have finished multiplying out the brackets, simplify by collecting like terms in order to pick up the final mark.

Multiplication of two brackets

Each term in the first bracket is multiplied by each term in the second bracket.
(Then simplify by collecting like terms.)

Examples
Expand and simplify the following:

a) $(x + 2)(x + 3)$ $= x(x + 3) + 2(x + 3)$
$= x^2 + 3x + 2x + 6$
$= x^2 + 5x + 6$

b) $(x + 5)(x - 3)$ $= x(x - 3) + 5(x - 3)$
$= x^2 - 3x + 5x - 15$
$= x^2 + 2x - 15$

c) $(x + y)^2$ $= x(x + y) + y(x + y)$
$= x^2 + xy + xy + y^2$
$= x^2 + 2xy + y^2$
(This is an identity; it is true for all values of x.)

A common error is to think that $(a + b)^2$ means $a^2 + b^2$.

Rearranging formulae

The **subject of a formula** is the letter that appears on its own on one side of the formula.

Examples
Make a the subject of these formulae:
a) $v = u + at$ b) $b = 3(a - 2)$

a) $v = u + at$
$v - u = at$ Subtract u from both sides.
$\dfrac{v - u}{t} = a$ Divide both sides by t.

So $a = \dfrac{v - u}{t}$ The subject of the formula is usually written first.

b) $b = 3(a - 2)$
$\dfrac{b}{3} = (a - 2)$ Divide both sides by 3.
$\dfrac{b}{3} + 2 = a$ Add 2 to both sides.

So $a = \dfrac{b}{3} + 2$

Factorisation (putting brackets in)

Factorisation is the reverse of **expanding brackets**. An expression is put into brackets by taking out **common factors**.

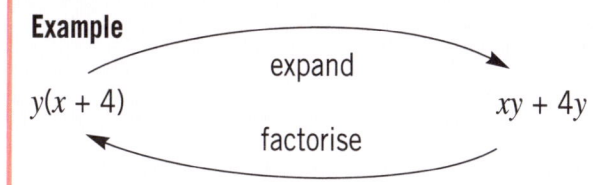

Example

$y(x + 4)$ — expand → $xy + 4y$
$xy + 4y$ — factorise → $y(x + 4)$

To factorise $xy + 4y$:
- Recognise that y is a factor of each term.
- Take out the common factor.
- The expression is completed inside the bracket, so that the result is equivalent to $xy + 4y$, when multiplied out.

Examples
Factorise the following expressions:

a) $4a + 8 = 4(a + 2)$
b) $3b + 6 = 3(b + 2)$
c) $3x^2 + 9 = 3(x^2 + 3)$
d) $5x^2 + x = x(5x + 1)$
e) $4m^2 + 8m = 4m(m + 2)$
f) $10a^2 - 15a = 5a(2a - 3)$
g) $12xy - 16x = 4x(3y - 4)$
h) $6x^3 + 18x^2 = 6x^2(x + 3)$
i) $\pi r^2 h + 2\pi r h = \pi r h(r + 2)$

Know the words

Formula – connects two expressions containing variables, the value of one variable depending on the values of the others. It must have an equals sign.
e.g. $v = u + at$ When the values of u, a, t are known, the value of v can be found using the formula.

Equation – connects two expressions, involving definite unknown values. It must have an equals sign.
e.g. $x + 2 = 5$ This is only true when $x = 3$.

Identity – connects expressions involving unspecified numbers. An identity always remains true, no matter what numerical values replace the letter symbols. It has an $\equiv$ sign.
e.g. $3(x + 2) \equiv 3x + 6$ This is true whatever the value of x.

Function – this is a relationship between two sets of values, such that the value from the first set maps onto a unique value in the second set.
e.g. $y = 4x - 1$ For any value of x, the value of y can be calculated.

KEY TERMS

Make sure you understand these terms before moving on!
- expanding brackets
- subject of a formula
- factorisation
- formula
- equation
- identity
- function

QUICK TEST

1. Multiply out the brackets and simplify where possible:
   a) $3(x + 2)$
   b) $2(x + y)$
   c) $-3(2x + 4)$
   d) $(x + 2)(x + 3)$
   e) $(y - 4)(y - 3)$
   f) $(a + 2)^2$

2. Factorise the following expressions:
   a) $6x - 18$
   b) $5y - 15$
   c) $5a + 20$
   d) $20x^2 + 10x$
   e) $15y - 20y^2$
   f) $20x^2y + 40xy$

3. Make b the subject of the formula $a = 5b - d$.

4. Make m the subject of the formula $y = mx + c$.

Equations 1

An *equation* involves an unknown value which has to be worked out.

Solving simple linear equations

An equation has two parts separated by an equals sign. When working out the unknown value in an equation, the **balance method** is used, that is, whatever you do to one side of an equation you must do the same to the other side.

Examples
Solve these equations.

a) $n - 7 = 10$
   $n = 10 + 7$ Add 7 to both sides.
   $n = 17$

b) $n + 6 = 8$
   $n = 8 - 6$ Subtract 6 from both sides.
   $n = 2$

c) $3n = 21$
   $n = \frac{21}{3}$ Divide both sides by 3.
   $n = 7$

d) $\frac{n}{4} = 3$
   $n = 3 \times 4$ Multiply both sides by 4.
   $n = 12$

Solving linear equations of the form $ax + b = c$

Remember, use the balance method; whatever is done to one side of the equation must be done to the other.

Examples

Solve these equations:

$2x + 15 = 9$
$\quad 2x = 9 - 15$ Subtract 15 from both sides.
$\quad 2x = -6$
$\quad\ x = -6 \div 2$ Divide both sides by 2.
$\quad\ x = -3$

Solve:

$\frac{n}{3} + 2 = 6$
$\quad \frac{n}{3} = 6 - 2$ Subtract 2 from both sides.
$\quad \frac{n}{3} = 4$
$\quad n = 4 \times 3$ Multiply both sides by 3.
$\quad n = 12$

Solving linear equations of the form $ax + b = cx + d$

The trick with this type of equation is to get the x's together on one side of the equals sign and the numbers on the other side.

Examples

Solve $6x - 4 = 4x + 8$
$6x - 4 - 4x = 8$ Subtract $4x$ from both sides.
$6x - 4x = 8 + 4$ Add 4 to both sides.
$2x = 12$
$x = \frac{12}{2}$ Divide each side by 2.
$x = 6$

Solve $5x - 9 = 12 - 4x$
$9x - 9 = 12$ Add $4x$ to both sides.
$9x = 21$ Add 9 to both sides.
$x = \frac{21}{9} = 2\frac{1}{3}$

> If in the exam you do not know that $\frac{21}{9} = 2\frac{1}{3}$, leave it as $\frac{21}{9}$. You will still get full marks!

Solving linear equations with brackets

Just because an equation has brackets don't be put off.
It's just the same as the other equations once the brackets have been multiplied out.

Examples

Solve:

a) $3(x - 4) = 21$
$3x - 12 = 21$ Multiply out the brackets first.
$3x = 21 + 12$ Then solve as before.
$3x = 33$
$x = \frac{33}{3}$
$x = 11$

b) $3(x - 2) = 2(x + 6)$
$3x - 6 = 2x + 12$
$3x - 6 - 2x = 12$
$x - 6 = 12$
$x = 12 + 6$
$x = 18$

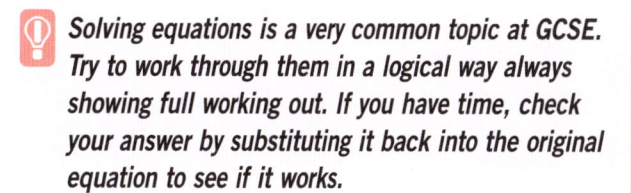

c) $5(n - 2) + 6 = 3(n - 4) + 10$
$5n - 10 + 6 = 3n - 12 + 10$
$5n - 4 = 3n - 2$
$2n = 2$
$n = 1$

> Solving equations is a very common topic at GCSE. Try to work through them in a logical way always showing full working out. If you have time, check your answer by substituting it back into the original equation to see if it works.

KEY TERMS

Make sure you understand this term before moving on!
- equation

QUICK TEST

Solve the following equations:
1. $x + 6 = 10$
2. $2x = 12$
3. $\frac{x}{5} = 4$
4. $x - 4 = 9$
5. $\frac{x}{2} - 3 = 9$
6. $4x + 2 = 20$
7. $5x + 3 = 2x + 9$
8. $6x - 1 = 15 + 2x$
9. $3(x + 2) = x + 4$
10. $2(x - 1) = 6(2x + 2)$

Equations 2

Using equations to solve problems

Example
The perimeter of the triangle is 20 cm.
Work out the value of x and hence find the lengths of the three sides.

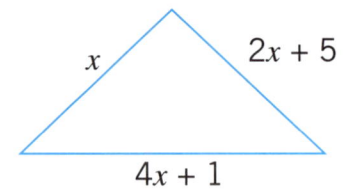

$$x + 2x + 5 + 4x + 1 = 20$$
$$7x + 6 = 20$$
$$7x = 20 - 6$$
$$7x = 14$$
$$x = \frac{14}{7}$$
$$x = 2$$

The perimeter is found by adding the lengths together.
Collect like terms and solve the equation as before.

So the lengths of the sides are 2 (= x), 9 (= $4x + 1$) and 9 (= $2x + 5$).

Example
Class 9B were playing a number game. Lucy said 'Multiplying a number by 3 and adding 6 gives the same answer as subtracting my number from 14'. What was Lucy's number?

- Call Lucy's number n and form an equation:
$3n + 6 = 14 - n$

- Solve the equation to work out Lucy's number.
$$3n + 6 = 14 - n$$
$$3n + 6 + n = 14$$
$$4n + 6 = 14$$
$$4n = 14 - 6$$
$$4n = 8$$
$$n = \frac{8}{4}$$
$$n = 2$$

Simultaneous equations

Two equations with two unknowns are called **simultaneous equations**. They can be solved in several ways. You only need to know how to solve them using a graphical method. Solving equations simultaneously involves finding values for the letters that will make both equations work.

Graphical method
The points at which any two graphs intersect represent the simultaneous solutions of their equations.

Example
Solve the simultaneous equations $y = 2x - 1$, $x + y = 5$.

- First draw the two graphs.

  $y = 2x - 1$ If $x = 0$, $y = -1$.
  If $y = 0$, $x = \frac{1}{2}$.
  If $y = 1$, $x = 1$.

  $x + y = 5$ If $x = 0$, $y = 5$.
  If $x = 5$, $y = 0$.

- This is the solution. At the point of intersection, $x = 2$ and $y = 3$.

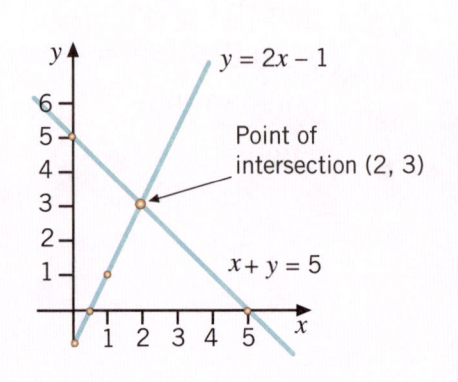

Solving cubic equations by trial and improvement

Trial and improvement is a method of solving equations by substituting values until a close value is found. This method is particularly useful when solving **cubic equations**.

Example
The equation $x^3 - 5x = 10$ has a solution between 2 and 3. Find this solution to 2 decimal places.

Draw up a table to help.
Substitute different values of x into $x^3 - 5x$.

x	$x^3 - 5x$	Comment
2.5	3.125	too small
2.8	7.952	too small
2.9	9.889	too small
2.95	10.922375	too big
2.94	10.712184	too big
2.91	10.092171	too big

At this stage we know the solution is somewhere between 2.90 and 2.91.
Checking the middle value, $x = 2.905$, gives $x^3 - 5x = 9.99036...$ which is too small.

```
      2.90            2.905           2.91
   (too small)     (too small)     (too big)
```

The diagram makes it clear that the solution is $x = 2.91$ correct to 2 decimal places.

> Make sure you write down the solution for x, not the answer to $x^3 - 5x$.

EQUATIONS 2 — Algebra

QUICK TEST

1. The diagram shows the graphs of the equations $x + y = 2$ and $y = x - 4$.
   Use the diagram to solve the simultaneous equations $x + y = 2$ and $y = x - 4$.

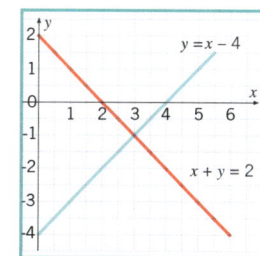

2. The equation $y^3 + y = 40$ has a solution between 3 and 4. Find this solution to 1 d.p. by using the method of trial and improvement. **(C)**

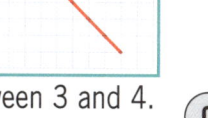

3. The width of a rectangle is x centimetres.
   The length of the rectangle is $(x + 2)$ centimetres.
   a) Find an expression in terms of x for the perimeter of the rectangle. Give your expression in its simplest form.
   b) The perimeter of the rectangle is 40 cm. Work out the length of the rectangle.

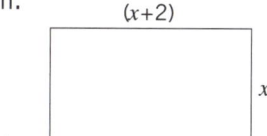

(C) Indicates that a calculator may be used.

KEY TERMS
Make sure you understand these terms before moving on!
- simultaneous equation
- trial and improvement
- cubic equation

Patterns, sequences, inequalities

A sequence is a list of numbers. There is usually a relationship between the numbers. Each value in the list is called a *term*.

Example
The odd numbers form a sequence 1, 3, 5, 7, 9, 11, . . . in which the terms have a *common difference* of 2.

1 →(+2)→ 3 →(+2)→ 5 →(+2)→ 7 →(+2)→ 9 →(+2)→ 11 . . .

Important number sequences
Square numbers   1, 4, 9, 16, 25, . . .   Triangular numbers   1, 3, 6, 10, 15, . . .
Cube numbers   1, 8, 27, 64, 125, . . .   The Fibonacci sequence   1, 1, 2, 3, 5, 8, 13, . . .

Dividing by 2, 5 and 10

One number is divisible by another if there is no remainder.

Examples
8 is divisible by 2
$8 \div 2 = 4$ (and no remainder)

17 is not divisible by 2
$17 \div 2 = 8$ remainder 1

- A number is divisible by 2 if it is an even number.
- A number is divisible by 5 if it ends in 0 or 5.
- A number is divisible by 10 if it ends in 0.

Finding the nth term of a linear sequence

The nth term is often denoted by U_n. For example, the 12th term is U_{12}.

For a **linear sequence**, the nth term takes the form $U_n = an + b$.

Example
Find an expression for the nth term of the sequence of odd numbers, 1, 3, 5, 7, 9, … .

- Find the common difference; this is a.
  Here $a = 2$. So $U_n = 2n + b$.
- Now substitute the values of U_1 and n.
  $n = 1$ and $U_1 = 1$
  This gives $1 = 2 + b$.
  So $b = -1$.
- nth term: $U_n = 2n - 1$
- Check: for the 5th term, $U_5 = 2 \times 5 - 1 = 9$ ✔

> 💡 *Check your rule for the nth term works by substituting another value of n into your expression.*

The nth term of a quadratic sequence

For a **quadratic sequence**, the first differences are not constant but the second differences are.

The nth term takes the form

$U_n = an^2 + bn + c$, where b, c may be zero.

Finding the nth term of a quadratic sequence can be a useful technique when you are carrying out investigational tasks for coursework.

Example
Find the nth term of 3, 9, 19, 33...

term (U_n)	1	2	3	4
number	3	9	19	33
1st difference		6	10	14
2nd difference			4	4

- a is found by dividing the second difference by 2.
- The nth term of this sequence is $2n^2 + 1$.

The four inequality symbols

$>$ means '**greater than**'
$<$ means '**less than**'
$\geq$ means '**greater than or equal to**'
$\leq$ means '**less than or equal to**'

So $x > 3$ and $3 < x$ both say 'x is greater than 3'.

Examples
Solve the following **inequalities**:

a) $x + 4 < 10$
   $x < 10 - 4$ Subtract 4 from both sides.
   $x < 6$

The solution of the inequality can be represented on a number line:

⟵————○————
          6

b) $4x - 2 \leq 2x + 6$
   $2x - 2 \leq 6$ Subtract $2x$ from both sides.
   $2x \leq 8$ Add 2 to both sides.
   $x \leq 4$ Divide both sides by 2.

The solution of the inequality can be represented on a number line:

⟵————●————
          4

Inequalities are solved in a similar way to equations. Multiplying and dividing by **negative numbers** changes the **direction** of the sign.

For example, if $-x \geq 5$ then $x \leq -5$.

c) $-5 < 3x + 1 \leq 13$ Subtract 1 from each part.
   $-6 < 3x \leq 12$ Divide each part by 3.
   $-2 < x \leq 4$

The **integer values** which satisfy the above inequality are **–1, 0, 1, 2, 3, 4.**

Use ○ when the end point is not included and ● when the end point is included.

KEY TERMS

Make sure you understand these terms before moving on!
- term
- common difference
- linear sequence
- inequality

QUICK TEST

1. Write the next two terms in each sequence.
   a) 5, 7, 9, 11,___ , ___
   b) 1, 4, 9, 16,___ , ___
   c) 12, 10, 8, 6,___ , ___

2. Write the nth term in each sequence.
   a) 5, 7, 9, 11, ...
   b) 2, 5, 8, 11, ...
   c) 6, 10, 14, 18, ...
   d) 8, 6, 4, 2, ...

3. Solve these inequalities.
   a) $2x - 3 < 9$
   b) $5x + 1 \geq 21$
   c) $1 \leq 3x - 2 \leq 7$
   d) $1 \leq 5x + 2 < 12$

Straight line graphs

Drawing straight line graphs

To draw a straight line graph, follow these easy steps:

Step 1
Choose 3 values of x and draw up a table.

Step 2
Work out the value of y for each value of x.

Step 3
Plot the coordinates and join up the points with a straight line.

Step 4
Label the graph.

Example
Draw the graph of $y = 3x - 1$.

1. Draw up a table with some suitable values of x.

x	−2	0	2
$y = 3x - 1$	−7	−1	5

2. Work out the y values by putting each x value into the equation.
   e.g. $x = -2$ ∴ $y = 3 \times -2 - 1$
   $= -6 - 1$
   $= -7$
3. Plot the points and draw the line.

Graphs of $y = a$, $x = b$

$y = a$ is a **horizontal** line with every y-coordinate equal to a.

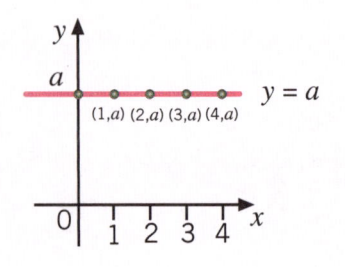

$x = b$ is a **vertical** line with every x-coordinate equal to b.

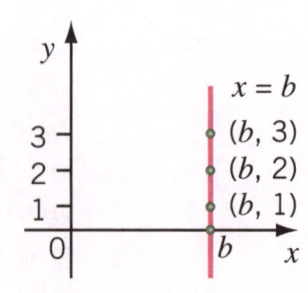

Finding the gradient of a line

- To find the **gradient**, choose two points on the line.
- Draw a triangle as shown.
- Find the change in y (height) and the change in x (base).
- gradient = $\dfrac{\text{change in } y}{\text{change in } x} = \dfrac{\text{height}}{\text{base}} = \dfrac{4}{3} = 1\dfrac{1}{3}$
- Decide if the gradient is positive or negative (see below).

Note: do not count the squares as the scales may be different.

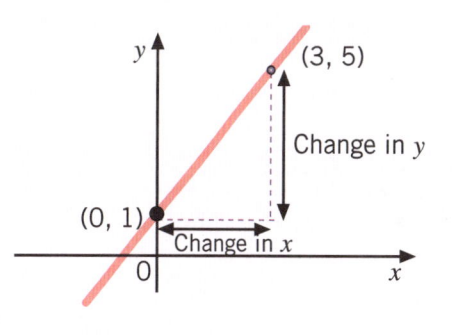

Interpreting $y = mx + c$

The general equation of a straight line graph is

$$y = mx + c.$$

m is the **gradient** (steepness) of the line.

- As m increases, the line gets steeper.
- If m is **positive**, the line slopes **forwards**.
- If m is **negative**, the line slopes **backwards**.

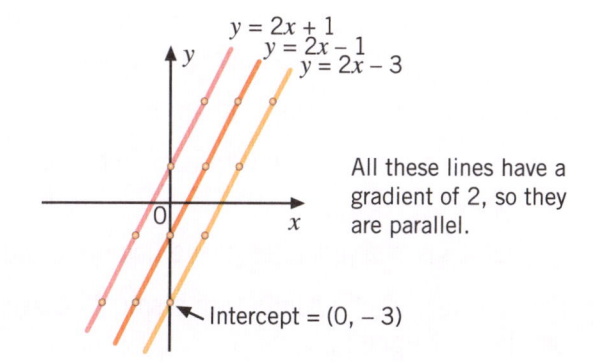

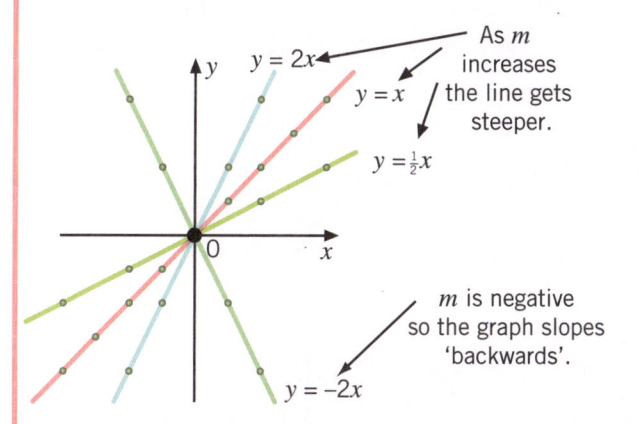

All these lines have a gradient of 2, so they are parallel.

Parallel lines have the **same gradient**.

c is the **intercept** on the y-axis, where the graph cuts the y-axis.

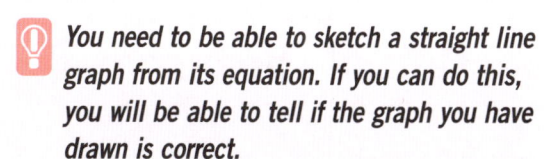

> You need to be able to sketch a straight line graph from its equation. If you can do this, you will be able to tell if the graph you have drawn is correct.

KEY TERMS

Make sure you understand these terms before moving on!
- horizontal
- vertical
- gradient
- intercept

QUICK TEST

1. Draw the graph of $y = 6 - 2x$. From your graph, write the solution of the equations:

   a) $6 - 2x = 4$ b) $6 - 2x = 3$

2. Write the gradient and intercept for each of these straight line graphs:

   a) $y = 4 + 2x$ b) $y = 3x - 2$ c) $2y = 6x + 4$

STRAIGHT LINE GRAPHS — Algebra

Curved graphs

Graphs of the form $y = ax^2 + b$

- These are curved graphs.

Example
Draw the graph of $y = x^2 - 3$.

x	-3	-2	-1	0	1	2	3
y	6	1	-2	-3	-2	1	6

- Work out the y-coordinates for several points.
- Remember that x^2 means x times x.
- Replace x in the equation with each coordinate, i.e. when $x = (-3)$, $y = (-3)^2 - 3 = 9 - 3 = 6$
- The table gives coordinates of the points for the graph.
- Plot and join up the points with a smooth curve and label the graph.

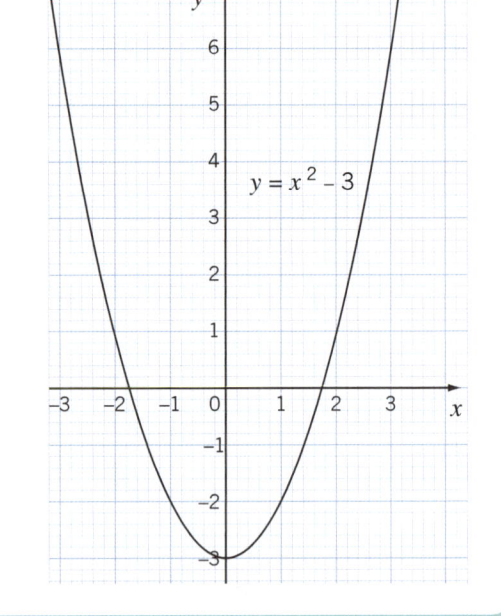

- If you are asked to draw the graph of $y = 2x^2$, remember this means $y = 2 \times (x^2)$.
(Square x first, then multiply by 2.)

Direction of the curve

If the number in front of x^2 is positive, the curve is U-shaped.

If the number in front of x^2 is negative, the curve is an upside-down U.

Graphs of the form $y = ax^2 + bx + c$

Example
Draw the graph of $y = x^2 - x - 6$ using values of x from –2 to 3.
Use the graph to find the value of x when $y = -3$.
- Make a table of values.

x	–2	–1	0	1	2	3	0.5
y	0	–4	–6	–6	–4	0	–6.25

$x = 0.5$ is worked out to find the minimum value.

- Work out the values of y by substituting the values of x into the equation:

  e.g. If $x = 1$, $\quad y = x^2 - x - 6$
  $\quad\quad\quad\quad\quad\quad = 1^2 - 1 - 6$
  $\quad\quad\quad\quad\quad\quad = -6$

- Don't try and punch this all into your calculator at once. Do it step by step.
- Plot the points and join them with a smooth curve.

- The **line of symmetry** is at $x = 0.5$.
- The **minimum value** is when $x = 0.5$, $y = -6.25$.
- The curve cuts the y-axis at $(0, -6)$, i.e. $(0, c)$.
- When $y = -3$, read across from $y = -3$ to the graph then read up to the x-axis: $x = -1.3$ and $x = 2.3$. These are the approximate solutions of the equation $x^2 - x - 6 = -3$.

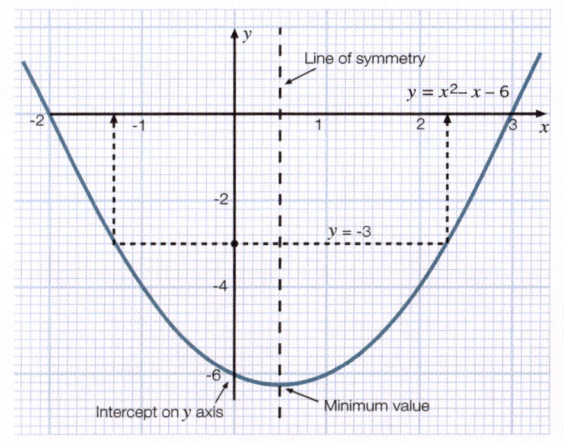

Show clearly on your graph how you take your readings.

> *Draw the curve with a sharp pencil. Go through all the points and check for any parts that look wrong.*

QUICK TEST

1 a) Complete the table of values for the graph $y = x^2 + 3$.

x	–3	–2	–1	0	1	2	3
y							

  b) Draw the graph of $y = x^2 + 3$.
  c) From the graph find the value of x when $y = 8$.

2 Complete the table of values and draw the graph of $y = 2x^2 - 1$ for values of x from –3 to 3.

x	–3	–2	–1	0	1	2	3
y							

Interpreting graphs

Graphs in practical situations

Linear graphs are often used to show **relationships**.

Example
The graph shows the charges made by a van hire firm.
- Point A shows how much was charged for hiring the van, i.e. £50.
- The gradient = 20.
  This means that £20 was charged per day for the hire of the van.

  Hence for 5 days' hire the van cost £50 + £20 × 5 = £150

Gradient = $\frac{120}{6}$ = 20

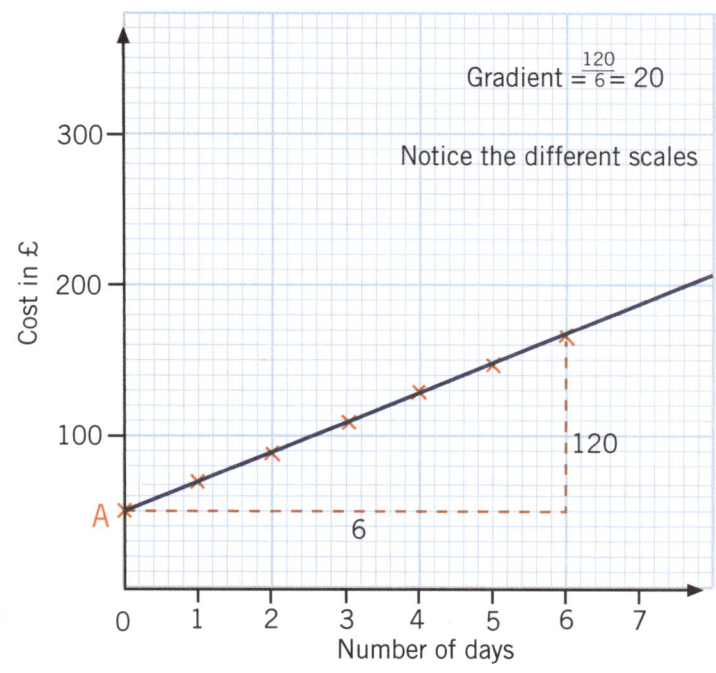

Notice the different scales

Distance–time graphs

These are often called **travel graphs**.
The **speed** of an object can be found by finding the gradient of the line:

$$\text{speed} = \frac{\text{distance travelled}}{\text{time taken}}$$

Example
The graph represents Mr Rogers' car journey. Work out the speed of each stage of the journey.
a) The car is travelling at 30 m.p.h. for 1 hour (30 ÷ 1).
b) The car is stationary for 30 minutes.
c) The graph is steeper so the car is travelling faster, at a speed of 60 m.p.h. for 30 minutes (30 ÷ 0.5).
d) The car is stationary for 1 hour.
e) The return journey is at a speed of 40 m.p.h. (60 ÷ 1.5).

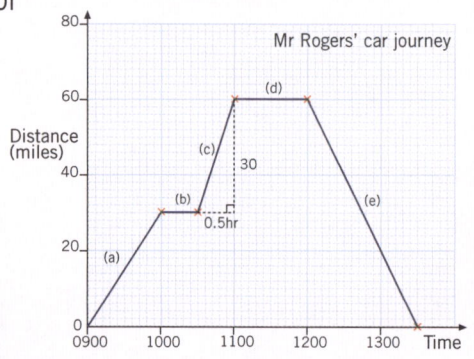

> *Notice the importance of using the gradient of a line. It is useful to note that on this distance–time graph example, the scales on the axes are different. Care must be taken when reading the scales: always make sure you understand the scales before you start.*

Conversion graphs

Coversion graphs are used to convert values of one quantity to another, e.g. litres to pints, km to miles, £ to dollars, etc.

Example
Suppose £1 is worth $1.50.
Draw a conversion graph.

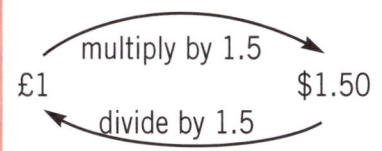

£1 —multiply by 1.5→ $1.50
$1.50 —divide by 1.5→ £1

- Make a table of values.

£	1	2	3	4	5
$	1.5	3.0	4.5	6.0	7.5

× 1.5

- Plot each of these points on the graph paper.
- To change $ to £, read across to the line then down, e.g. $4 is £2.67 (approx.).
- To change £ to $, read up to the line then across, e.g. £4.50 is $6.80 (approx.).

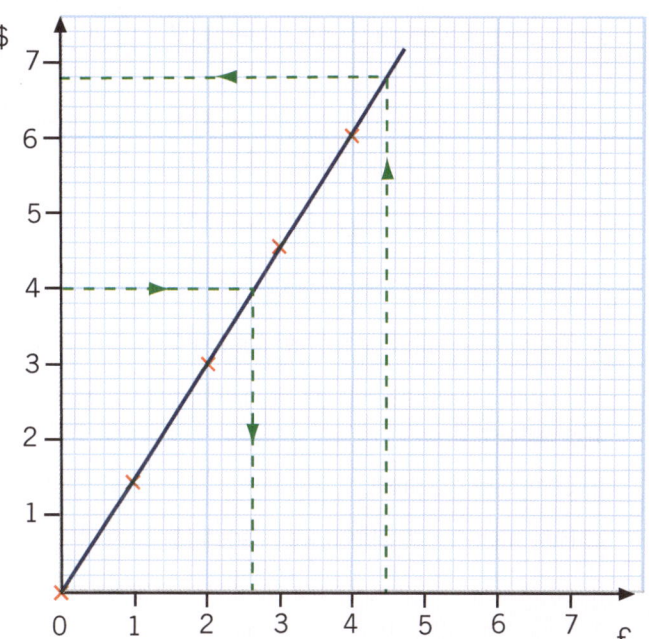

QUICK TEST

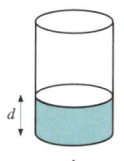

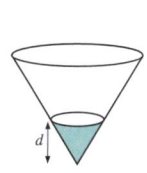

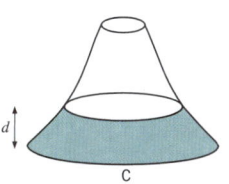

1 These containers are being filled with a liquid at a rate of 150 ml per second.

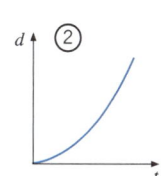

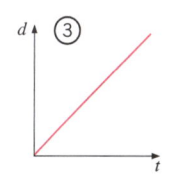

A, B, C containers; graphs ①, ②, ③

The graphs show how the depth of the water changes with time. Match the containers with the graphs.

2 The travel graph shows the car journeys of two people. From the travel graph find:

a) the speed at which Miss Young is travelling

b) the length of time Mr Price has a break

c) the speed of Mr Price from London to Birmingham

d) the time at which Miss Young and Mr Price pass each other

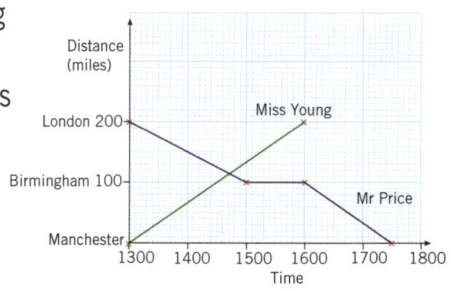

KEY TERMS
Make sure you understand these terms before moving on!
- travel graph
- speed
- conversion graph

INTERPRETING GRAPHS — Algebra

Practice questions

Use the questions to test your progress.
Check your answers on page 93.

1. Write down a formula for the total cost T, in pence, of y balloons at 85 pence each and 8 party poppers at z pence each.

   ....

2. Here are some patterns made out of matchsticks:

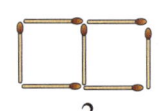

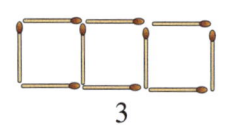

   1   2   3   4

   a) In the space provided, draw pattern 4.

   The table shows the number of matchsticks needed for pattern 1 to pattern 3.

   b) Complete the table.

   c) How many matchsticks are needed for pattern 100?

   d) Write down a formula connecting the pattern number (p) and the number of matchsticks (m).

Pattern number	Number of matchsticks
1	4
2	7
3	10
4	
5	
6	

3. Solve these equations.
   a) $n + 5 = 12$ b) $n - 6 = 8$ c) $5n = 35$ d) $\frac{n}{3} = 6$

   ....

4. Multiply out these brackets.
   a) $5(n + 2)$ b) $3(n - 2)$ c) $2(n - 5)$ d) $-3(n - 6)$

   ....

5. Write down the next two numbers in this sequence: 5, 9, 13, 17, ..., ...

6. Solve the following equations.
   a) $2x + 4 = 10$ b) $3x - 1 = 11$ c) $5x - 3 = 2x + 12$ d) $3(x + 1) = 9$ e) $2(x + 1) = x + 3$

   ....

7. The perimeter of the triangle is 22 cm.
   a) Write an equation for the perimeter of the triangle.
   b) Use your equation to find the length of the shortest side of the triangle.

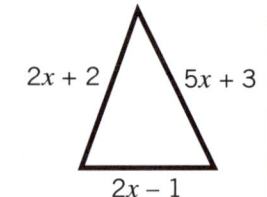

   Sides: $2x + 2$, $5x + 3$, $2x - 1$

   ....

8. a) Complete this table of values for $y = 3x - 4$.

x	-2	-1	0	1	2	3
$y = 3x - 4$			-4			

   b) On graph paper, plot your values for x and y. Join your points with a straight line.
   c) Write down the coordinates of the points where your line crosses the x-axis.

9. Here are the first five terms of a number sequence: 3, 9, 19, 33, 51.
   Write down an expression for the nth term of the sequence.

   ....

10. Simplify these expressions by collecting like terms.
    a) $a + a + a + a$
    b) $2b + 3b$
    c) $5b - 2b$
    d) $3c - 2c + 5c$
    e) $6a + 3b - 4b + 2a$

11. Factorise the following expressions.
    a) $5a - 10$
    b) $6b + 12$
    c) $8y^2 + 12y$

12. Simplify:
    a) $x^5 \times x^2$
    b) $6^{10} \div 6^7$
    c) $3x^2 \times 4x^3$

13. If $a = b^2 - 6$
    a) calculate the value of a if $b = 3$.
    b) calculate the value of a if $b = -4$.

14. $P^2 = 5xy - 3x^2$
    a) Calculate the value of P when $x = 5.8$, $y = 105$. (C)
    b) Rearrange the formula $P^2 = 5xy - 3x^2$ to make y the subject.

15. The equation $x^3 - 2x = 2$ has a solution between 1 and 2.
    By using a method of trial and improvement, find this solution to 1 decimal place. (C)

16. Solve the inequality $2 \leqslant 5n - 3 \leqslant 12$.

17. Water is being poured into these containers at a rate of 250 ml per second. The graphs below show how the height of the water changes with time. Match the containers with the graphs.

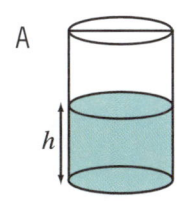

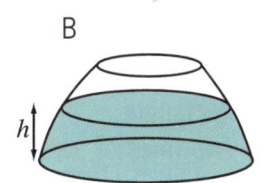

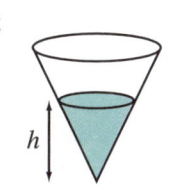

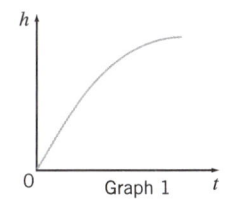

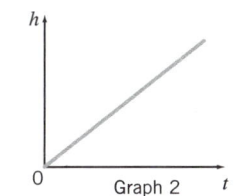

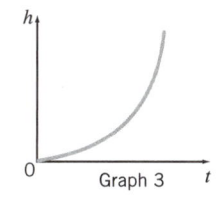

    A   B   C

    Graph 1   Graph 2   Graph 3

18. Write down the nth term of the linear sequence: 3, 7, 11, 15, 19, ...

(C) *Indicates that a calculator may be used.*

How well did you do? ✗ 1–7 Try again   8–12 Getting there   13–16 Good work   17–18 Excellent! ✓

Shapes

The circle

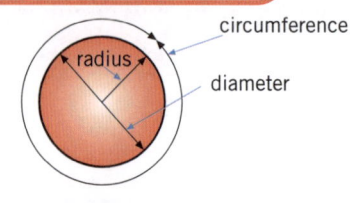

Diameter = 2 × **radius**.

The **circumference** is the distance around the outside edge.

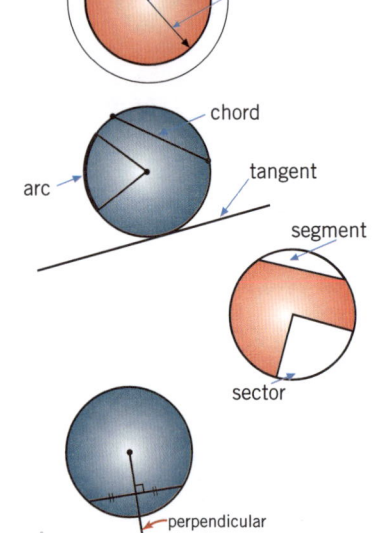

A **chord** is a line that joins two points on the circumference.
A chord that goes through the centre is a diameter.
A **tangent** touches the circle at one point only.
An **arc** is part of the circumference.

A **sector** is a part of a circle enclosed between two radii.

A **segment** is formed when chords divide the circle into different parts.

The **perpendicular bisector** of any chord passes through the centre of the circle.

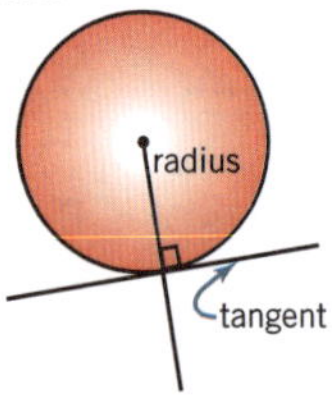

The radius and tangent at a point make an angle of 90°.

Quadrilaterals

These are four-sided shapes. You need to be able to sketch these shapes and know their symmetrical properties.

Square
Four lines of symmetry
Rotational symmetry of order 4

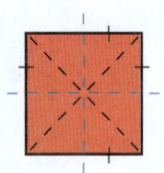

Rectangle
Two lines of symmetry
Rotational symmetry of order 2

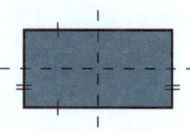

Parallelogram
No lines of symmetry
Rotational symmetry of order 2

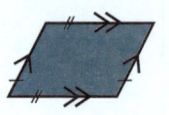

Rhombus
Two lines of symmetry
Rotational symmetry of order 2

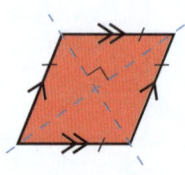

Kite
One line of symmetry
No rotational symmetry

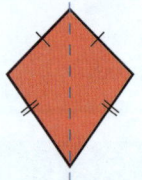

Trapezium
Isosceles trapezium:
One line of symmetry
No rotational symmetry

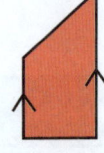

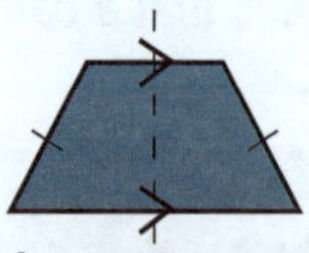

Parallel lines are the lines that remain the same distance apart, i.e. they never meet.

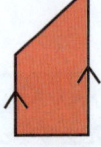

isosceles trapezium

No lines of symmetry
No rotational symmetry
trapezium

Polygons

These are 2D shapes with straight sides. Regular **polygons** are shapes with all sides and angles equal.

Number of sides	Name of polygon
3	Triangle
4	Quadrilateral
5	Pentagon
6	Hexagon
7	Heptagon
8	Octagon

> *Try to learn all the shapes and their symmetrical properties.*

Regular pentagon
- five equal sides
- rotational symmetry of order 5
- five lines of symmetry

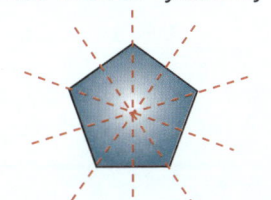

Regular hexagon
- six equal sides
- rotational symmetry of order 6
- six lines of symmetry

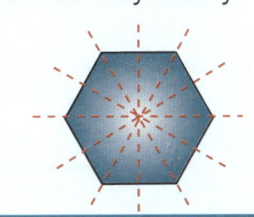

Regular octagon
- eight equal sides
- rotational symmetry of order 8
- eight lines of symmetry

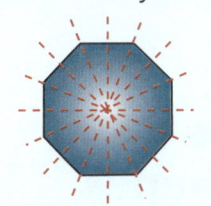

Triangles

There are several types of triangle.

Right-angled
Has a 90° angle

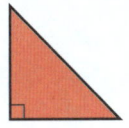

Equilateral
Three sides equal
Three angles equal

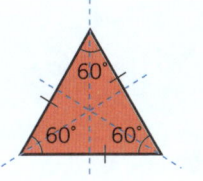

Isosceles
Two sides equal
Base angles equal

Scalene
No sides or angles the same

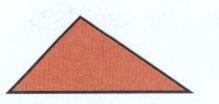

KEY TERMS

Make sure you understand these terms before moving on!
- diameter
- radius
- circumference
- chord
- tangent
- arc
- sector
- segment
- polygon

QUICK TEST

1. What is the name of a six-sided polygon?

2. From memory, draw all the main types of triangles and quadrilaterals.

Solids

Plans and elevations

A **plan** is what is seen if a 3D shape is viewed from above.
An **elevation** is seen if the 3D shape is viewed from the side or front.

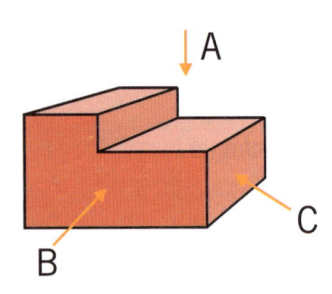

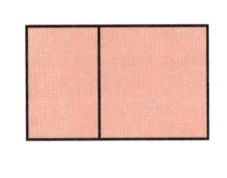

plan A

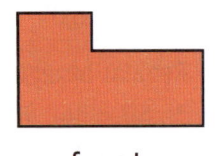

front elevation B

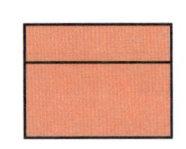

side elevation C

3D shapes

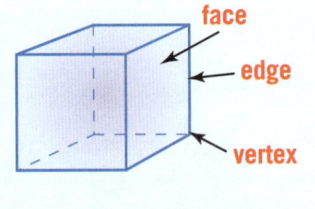

face
edge
vertex

cube

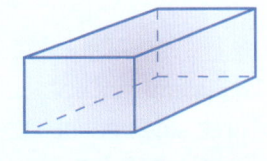

cuboid

sphere

cylinder

A cuboid has 6 faces, 8 vertices and 12 edges

cone

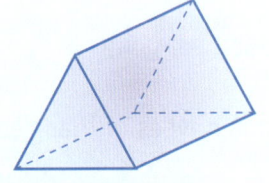

triangular prism

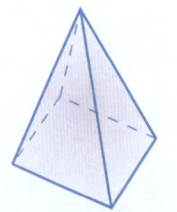

square-based pyramid

A prism is a solid that can be cut into slices which are all the same shape.

Remember to learn the mathematical names of the solids.

Isometric drawings

Examples
a) You can represent 3D shapes on **isometric paper**. On this paper you can draw lengths in three perpendicular directions on the same scale. The faces do not appear in their true shapes.
b) The 'T' shaped prism can be shown clearly on isometric paper.

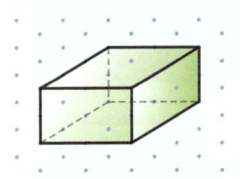

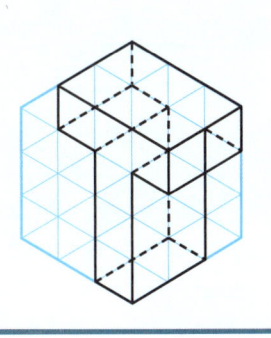

Nets of solids

The **net** of a 3D shape is the 2D (flat) shape, that can be folded to make the 3D shape.

Examples

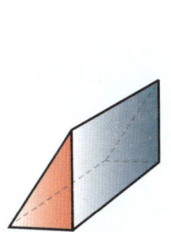

cuboid

net

triangular prism

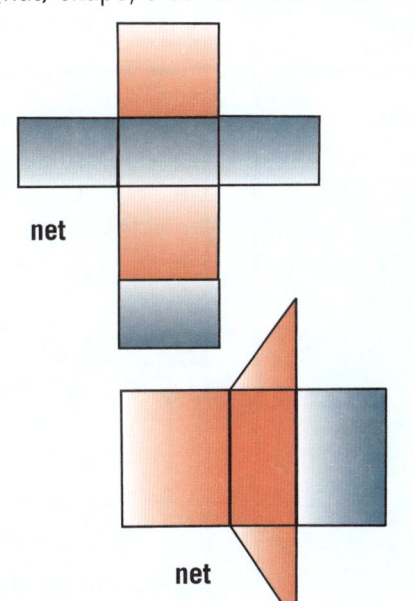

net

When asked to draw an accurate net, you must measure carefully.

When making the shape, remember to put tabs on, to stick it together.

SOLIDS — Shape, space and measures

KEY TERMS

Make sure you understand these terms before moving on!
- plan
- elevation
- vertex
- edge
- face
- net

QUICK TEST

1. Draw an accurate net of this 3D shape.

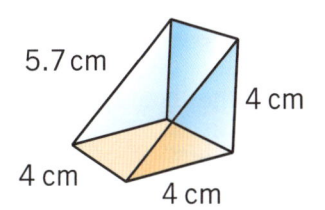

   5.7 cm, 4 cm, 4 cm, 4 cm

2. Draw a sketch of the plan and elevations from A and B of this solid

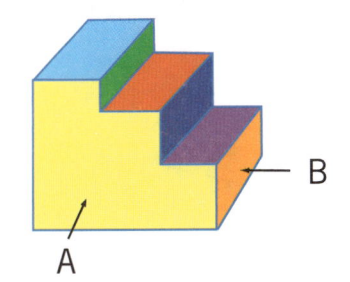

51

Symmetry

Reflective symmetry

Reflective symmetry is when both sides of a symmetrical shape are the same when the mirror line is drawn across it. The mirror line is known as the **line** or **axis of symmetry**.

1 line of symmetry   1 line of symmetry   3 lines of symmetry   No lines of symmetry

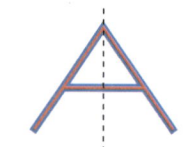

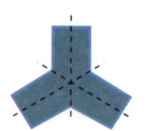

Rotational symmetry

A 2D (two-dimensional) shape has rotational symmetry if, when turned about the centre, it looks exactly the same. The **order of rotational symmetry** is the number of times the shape looks the same within one complete turn (360°). For the letter M, the shape has 1 such position. It is said to have **rotational symmetry of order 1**, or no rotational symmetry. The same is true for letter T.

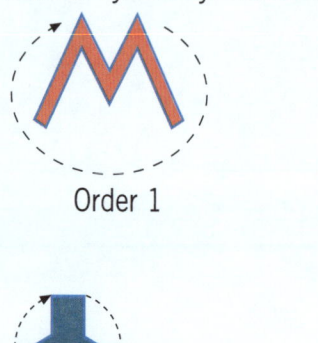

Order 1   Order 1

Order 3 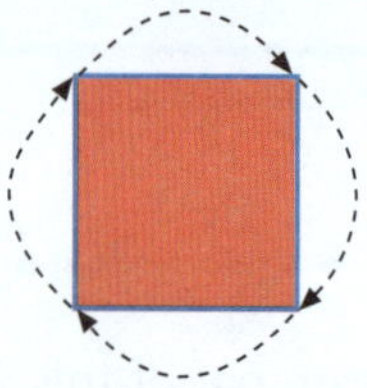   Order 4

Plane symmetry

Only 3D (three-dimensional) solids have this type of symmetry.

A 3D shape has a **plane of symmetry** if the plane divides the shape into two halves, and one half is an exact mirror image of the other.

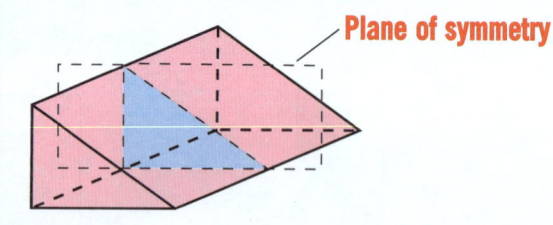

Plane of symmetry

When asked to draw in a plane of symmetry on a solid, make sure that it is a closed shape – don't just draw in a line of symmetry.

QUICK TEST

1. What are the names of the three types of symmetry?
2. The dashed lines are the lines of symmetry. Complete the shape so that it is symmetrical.
3. Draw a plane of symmetry on this solid.

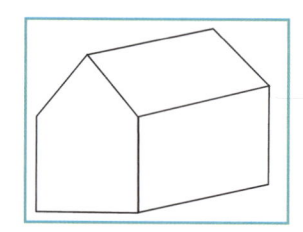

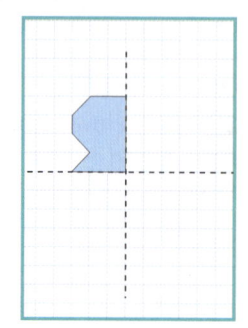

KEY TERMS

Make sure you understand these terms before moving on!
- reflective symmetry
- axis of symmetry
- rotational symmetry
- plane of symmetry

Constructions

Constructing a triangle

Example
Use compasses to construct this triangle.
- Draw the longest side.
- With the compass point at A, draw an arc of radius 4 cm.
- With the compass point at B, draw an arc of radius 5 cm.
- Join A and B to the point where the two arcs meet at C.

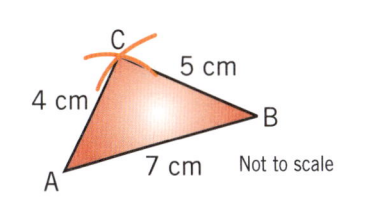

The perpendicular bisector of a line

- Draw a line segment XY.
- Draw two arcs with the compasses, using X as the centre. The compasses must be set at a radius greater than half the distance of XY.
- Keeping the compasses the same distance apart draw two more arcs with Y as the centre.
- Join the two points where the arcs cross (A and B).
- AB is the **perpendicular bisector** of XY.
- N is the **midpoint** of XY.

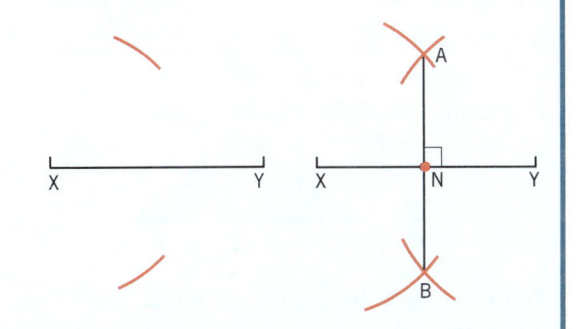

The perpendicular from a point to a line

From P draw arcs to cut the line at A and B.
From A and B draw arcs with the same radius to intersect C.
Join P to C; this line is perpendicular to AB.

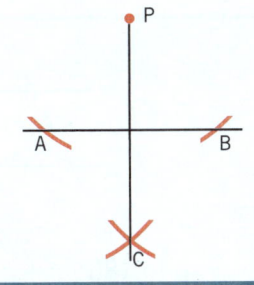

The perpendicular from a point on a straight line

Construct the perpendicular at the point N on a line.
- With the compasses set to a radius of about 4 cm, and centred on N, draw arcs to cut the line at A and B.
- Construct the perpendicular bisector of the line segment AB as shown.

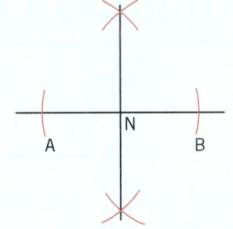

Bisecting an angle

- Draw two lines XY and YZ to meet at an angle.
- With the compass point at Y draw the two arcs on XY and YZ.
- Place the compass point at the two arcs and draw arcs to cross at N.
- Join Y and N. YN is the **bisector** of angle XYZ.

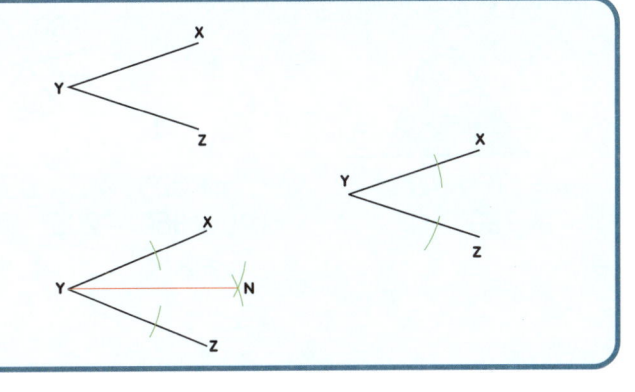

Angles

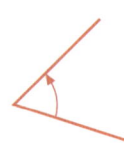

An *acute angle* is between 0° and 90°.

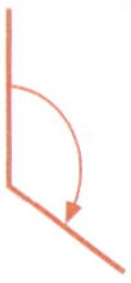

An *obtuse angle* is between 90° and 180°.

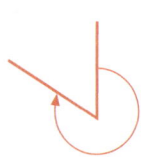

A *reflex angle* is between 180° and 360°.

A *right angle* is 90°.

Angle facts

Angles on a **straight line** add up to **180°**.
$a + b + c = 180°$

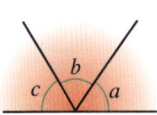

Angles at a **point** add up to **360°**.
$a + b + c + d = 360°$

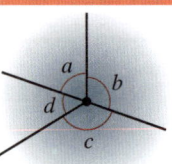

Angles in a **triangle** add up to **180°**.
$a + b + c = 180°$

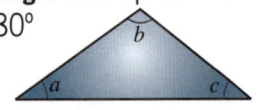

Angles in a **quadrilateral** add up to **360°**.
$a + b + c + d = 360°$

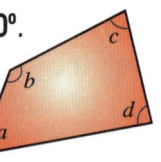

Vertically opposite angles are **equal**.
$a = b, c = d$
$a + d = b + c = 180°$

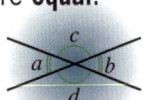

An **exterior angle** of a triangle equals the sum of the **two** opposite interior angles. $a + b = c$

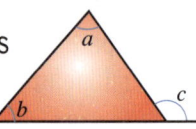

Reading angles

When asked to find XYZ or ∠XYZ or XŶZ, find the angle labelled with the **middle letter**, angle Y.

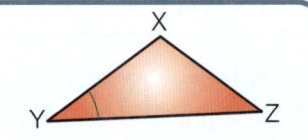

Angles in parallel lines

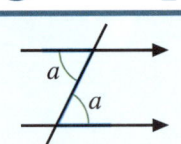

Alternate (z) angles are **equal**.

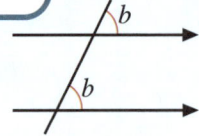

Corresponding angles are **equal**.

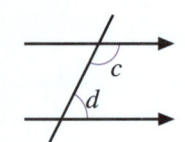

Supplementary angles add up to **180°**: $c + d = 180°$

Examples
Find the angles labelled by letters.

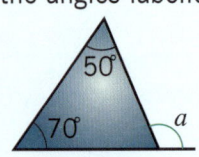

$a = 50° + 70°$
$= 120°$

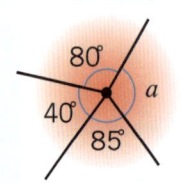

$a + 80° + 40° + 85° = 360°$
$a = 360° - 205°$
$= 155°$

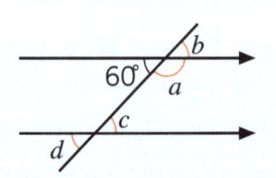

$a = 120°$ (angles on a straight line)
$b = 60°$ (vertically opposite)
$c = 60°$ (corresponding to b or alternate to 60°)
$d = 60°$ (vertically opposite to c)

Measuring angles

A protractor is used to measure the size of an angle.

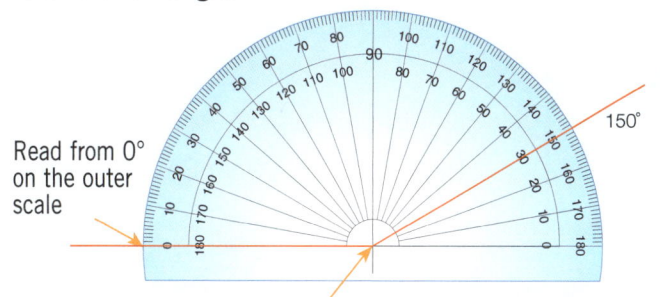

Read from 0° on the outer scale

Place the cross at the point of the angle you are measuring

For the above angle, measure on the outer scale since you must start from 0°.

> *Beware, make sure you put the 0° line at the start position and read from the correct scale. When measuring angles, count the degree lines carefully and always double check.*

Tesselations

A **tessellation** is a pattern of 2D shapes which fit together without leaving any gaps.

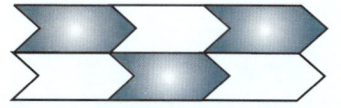

For shapes to tessellate, the angles at each point must add up to 360°.

Example
Regular pentagons will not tessellate.
Each interior angle is 108°, and
$3 \times 108° = 324°$.
A gap of $360° - 324° = 36°$ is left.

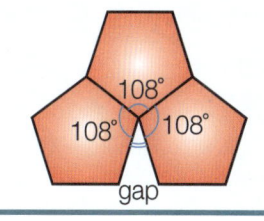

Angles in a polygon

There are two types of angle in a polygon: **interior** (inside) and **exterior** (outside).
For a regular polygon with n sides:
- sum of exterior angles = 360°, so exterior angle = $\frac{360°}{n}$
- interior angle + exterior angle = 180°
- sum of interior angles = $(n - 2) \times 180°$ or $(2n - 4) \times 90°$.

Example
A regular polygon has an interior angle of 150°.
How many sides does it have?
Let n be the number of sides.
exterior + interior = 180°
So exterior angle = 180° − 150° = 30°
But exterior angle = $\frac{360°}{n}$
So $n = \frac{360°}{\text{exterior angle}}$
$n = \frac{360°}{30°} = 12$

> *Make sure that you show full working out when carrying out an angle calculation. If you are asked to 'Explain', always refer to the angle properties, e.g. angles on a straight line add up to 180°, rather than how you worked it out.*

KEY TERMS

Make sure you understand these terms before moving on!
- acute angle
- obtuse angle
- reflex angle
- alternate angle
- corresponding angle
- supplementary angle
- tessellation

QUICK TEST

1. Find the sizes of the angles below labelled by letters.
   a. (30°)
   b. (110°)
   c. (50°)

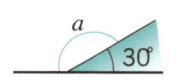

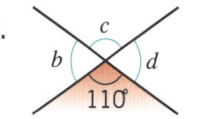

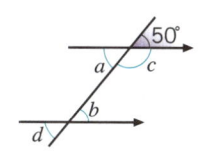

2. Find the size of an a) exterior and b) interior angle of a regular pentagon.

ANGLES

Shape, space and measures

55

Bearings and scale drawings

Bearings

- A bearing is the direction travelled between two points, given as an angle in degrees.
- All bearings are measured clockwise from the north line.
- All bearings should be given as 3 figures, e.g. 225°, 043°, 006°.

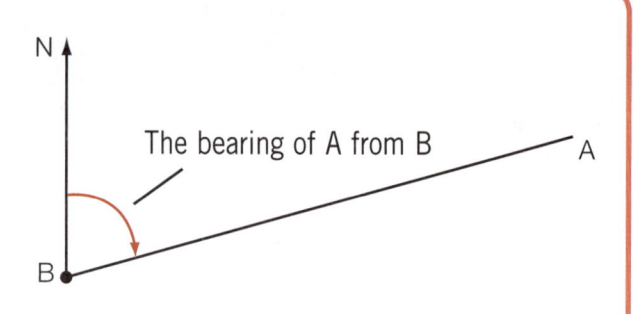

The bearing of A from B

Examples

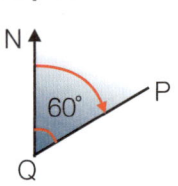

Bearing of P from Q = 060°

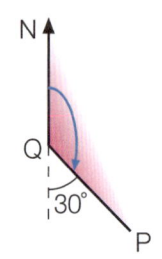

Bearing of P from Q = 180° − 30° = 150°

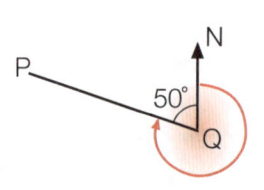

Bearing of P from Q = 360° − 50° = 310°

Always measure from the north line at Q.

Back bearings

To find the back bearing (the bearing of Q from P in the examples above):
- First draw in a north line at P.
- The two north lines are parallel lines, so you can use the angle properties of parallel lines.

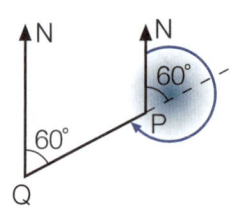

Bearing of Q from P = 60° + 180° = 240°

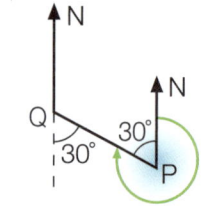

Bearing of Q from P = 360° − 30° = 330°

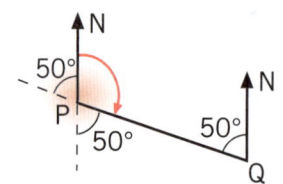

Bearing of Q from P = 180° − 50° = 130°

Measure from the north lines at P.

Scale drawings and bearings

Scale drawings are used for finding lengths and angles.

The word 'from' is important when answering bearing questions. It tells you where to put the north line and where to measure.

Example

A ship sails from a harbour for 15 km on a bearing of 040°, and then continues due east for 20 km. Make a scale drawing of this journey using a scale of 1 cm to 5 km. How far will the ship have to sail to get back to the harbour by the shortest route? What will the bearing be?

Shortest route = 6.4 × 5 km = 32 km
Bearing = 70° + 180° = 250°

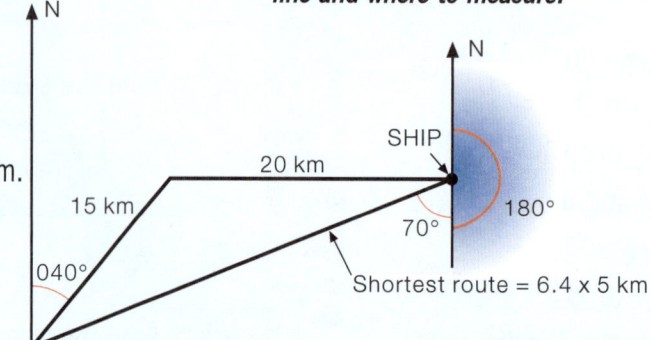

Shortest route = 6.4 × 5 km

This diagram is not drawn accurately but is used to show you what your diagram should look like.

Scales and maps

Scales are often used on maps. They are usually written as a ratio.

Example
The scale on a road map is 1 : 25 000. Bury and Oldham are 20 cm apart on the map.
Work out the real distance, in km, between Bury and Oldham.

Scale 1 : 25 000, distance on map is 20 cm.
  Real distance = 20 × 25 000 = 500 000 cm

Divide by 100 to change cm to m.
  500 000 ÷ 100 = 5000 m

Divide by 1000 to change m to km.
  5000 ÷ 1000 = 5 km

A scale of 1 : 25 000 means that 1 cm on the scale drawing represents a real length of 25 000 cm.

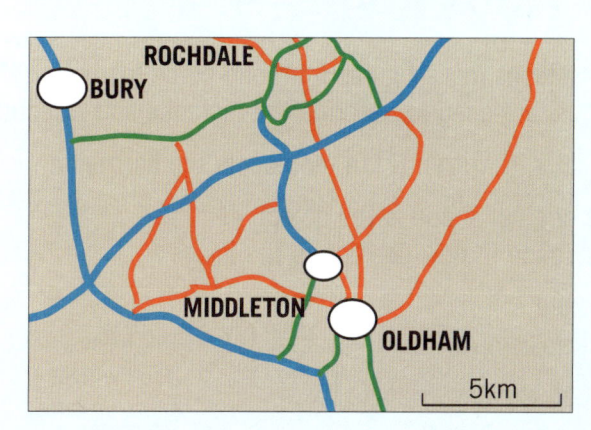

QUICK TEST

1. What are the bearings of A from B in the following diagrams:

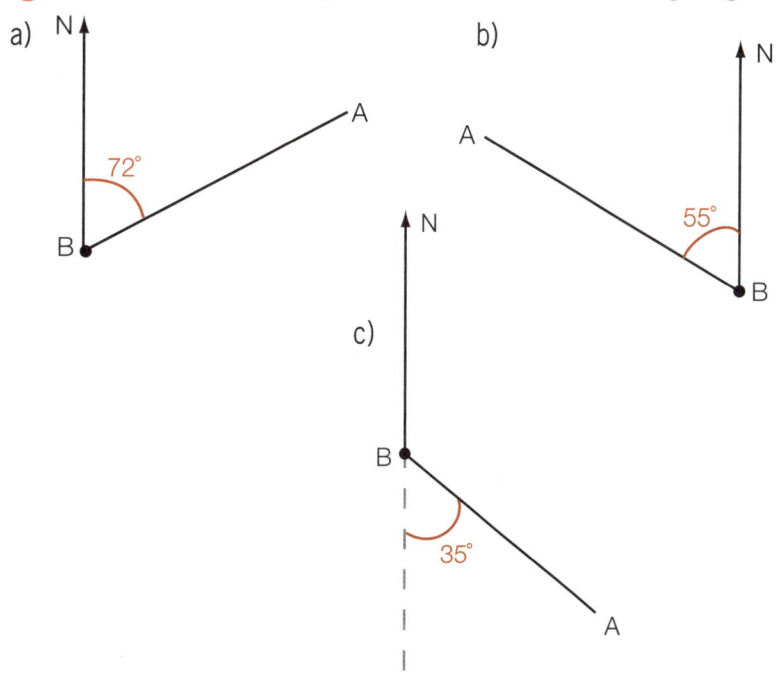

   a) 72°

   b) 55°

   c) 35°

2. For each of the questions above work out the bearing of B from A.

3. The scale on a road map is 1 : 50 000.
   If two towns are 14 cm apart on the map, work out the real distance between them.

BEARINGS AND SCALE DRAWINGS

Shape, space and measures

Transformations 1

A transformation changes the position or size of a shape.
There are four types of transformations:
translations, reflections, rotations and *enlargements*.

Translations

Translations move figures from one place to another. The size and shape of the figure are not changed.
Vectors are used to describe the distance and direction of the translation.

A vector is written $\binom{a}{b}$. **a** represents the **horizontal** movement, and **b** represents the **vertical** movement.

The original shape is the object.
The shape in new position is the **image**.

Example

a) Translate ABC by the vector $\binom{2}{1}$.   This means
   Call the new triangle P.   2 to the right
                                                  and 1 upwards.

b) Translate ABC by the vector $\binom{-3}{-2}$. This means
   Call the new triangle Q.   3 to the left
                                                  and 2 down.

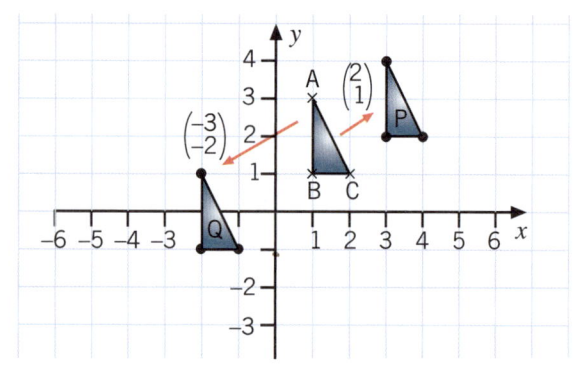

P and Q are **congruent** – two shapes are congruent if they are exactly the same size and shape.

Reflections

Reflections create an image of an object on the other side of the mirror line. The mirror line is known as an **axis of reflection**. The size and shape of the figure are not changed.

Example
Reflect triangle ABC in:
a) the *x* axis, and call the image D.
b) the line $y = -x$, and call the image E.
c) the line $x = 5$, and call the image F.

D, E and F are congruent to triangle ABC.

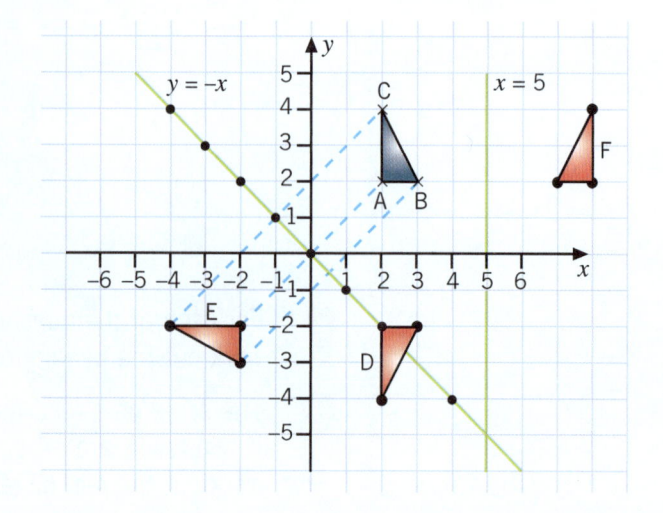

> *Count the squares to find the distance from the object to the mirror.*

Rotations

Rotations turn a figure through an angle about some fixed point. This fixed point is called the **centre of rotation**. The size and shape of the figure are not changed.

Example
Rotate triangle ABC:
a) 90° clockwise about (0, 0) and call it R.
b) 180° about (0, 0), and call it S.
c) 90° anticlockwise about (–1, 1), and call it T.

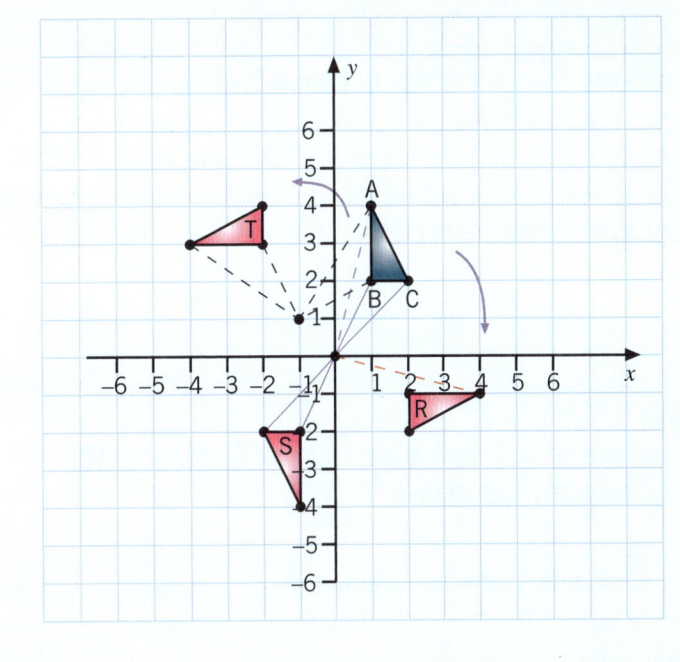

When describing a rotation give:
- the centre of rotation
- the direction of the turn (clockwise/anticlockwise)
- the angle of the turn

Otherwise you will lose marks for not describing them fully.

QUICK TEST

1 On the diagram below:

a) Translate ABC by the vector $\begin{pmatrix} -3 \\ 1 \end{pmatrix}$. Call it P.
b) Reflect ABC in the line $y = x$. Call it Q.
c) Reflect ABC in the line $y = -1$. Call it R.
d) Rotate ABC 180° about (0, 0). Call it S.

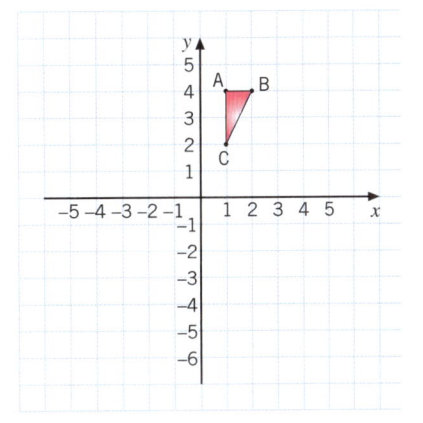

2 What does the vector $\begin{pmatrix} -2 \\ 3 \end{pmatrix}$ mean?

KEY TERMS

Make sure you understand these terms before moving on!
- translation
- reflection
- rotation
- enlargement
- vector
- congruent

Transformations 2

Enlargements

Enlargements change the size but not the shape of an object.
The **centre of enlargement** is the point from which the enlargement takes place.
The **scale factor** indicates how many times the lengths of the original figure have changed size.
- If the scale factor is **greater than 1**, the shape becomes **bigger**.
- If the scale factor is **less than 1**, the shape becomes **smaller**.

Example
Enlarge triangle ABC by a scale factor of 2, centre = (0, 0).
Call the enlarged triangle A'B'C'.

Notice each side of the enlargement is twice the size of the corresponding side in the original. A'B' = 2AB

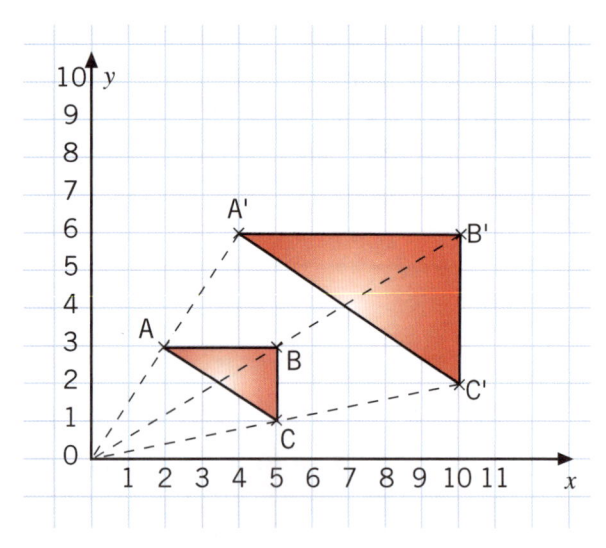

Example
Describe fully the transformation that maps ABCDEF onto A'B'C'D'E'F'.
- To find the centre of enlargement, join A to A', and continue the line.
  Join B to B', and continue the line. Do the same for the vertices.
- Where all the lines meet is the centre of enlargement, (–1, 3).
- The transformation is an enlargement with scale factor $\frac{1}{3}$.
  The centre of enlargement is at (–1, 3).

Notice that A'B'C'D'E'F' is a third of the size of ABCDEF.

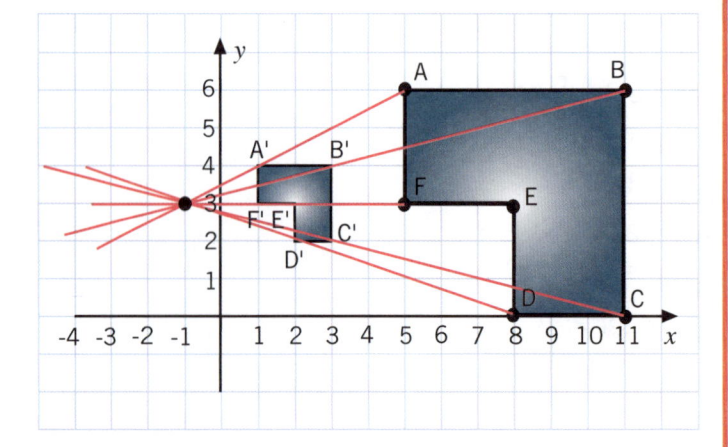

> When asked to describe an enlargement, you must include the scale factor and the position of the centre of enlargement.

Combining transformations

Combined transformations are a series of two or more transformations.

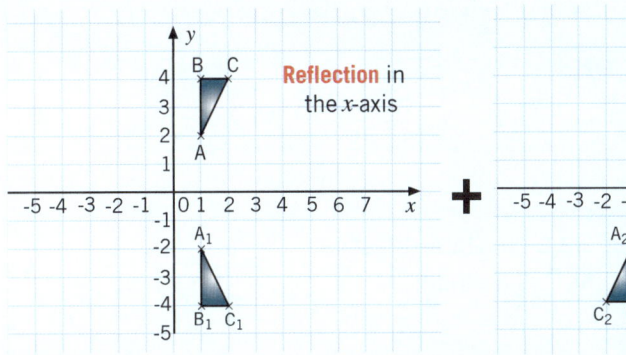

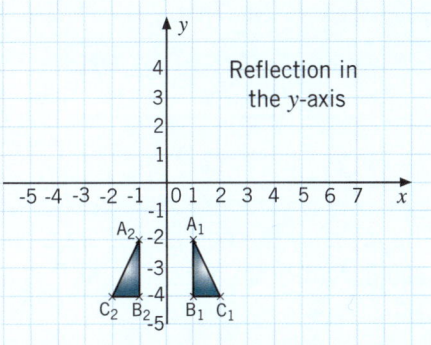

Reflection in the x-axis + *Reflection in the y-axis*

Example
For triangle ABC:
a) Reflect ABC in the x-axis. Call the image $A_1B_1C_1$.
b) Reflect $A_1B_1C_1$ in the y-axis. Call the image $A_2B_2C_2$.

The single transformation that maps ABC directly onto $A_2B_2C_2$ is a rotation of 180° about centre (0, 0).

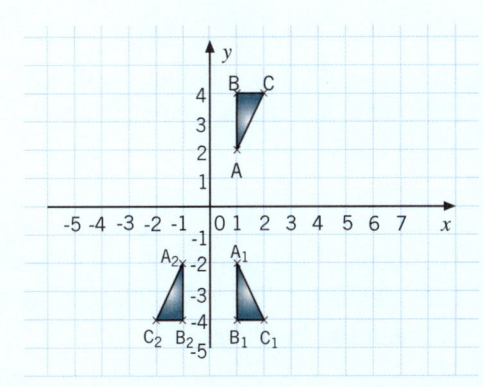

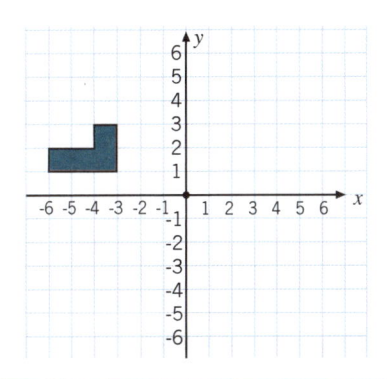

KEY TERMS

Make sure you understand these terms before moving on!
- centre of enlargment
- scale factor
- reflection

QUICK TEST

1. Draw an enlargement of shape P with a scale factor of 2, centre of enlargement as shown.

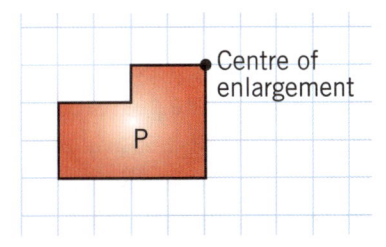

2. a) Rotate the shaded shape through a 90° clockwise rotation about (0, 0). Call this shape B.
   b) Reflect shape B in the x axis and call this shape C.

TRANSFORMATIONS 2

Shape, space and measures

61

Loci and coordinates

The *locus* of a point is the set of all the possible positions which that point can occupy, subject to some given condition or rule.
The plural of locus is *loci*.

Common loci

- The locus of the points that are a constant distance (**equidistant**) from a fixed point P is a circle.

- The locus of the points that are equidistant from two points X and Y is the **perpendicular bisector** of the line XY.

- The locus of the points that are equidistant from two lines is the line which bisects the angle between the two lines.

- The locus of the points that are a constant distance from a line XY is a pair of parallel lines above and below XY.

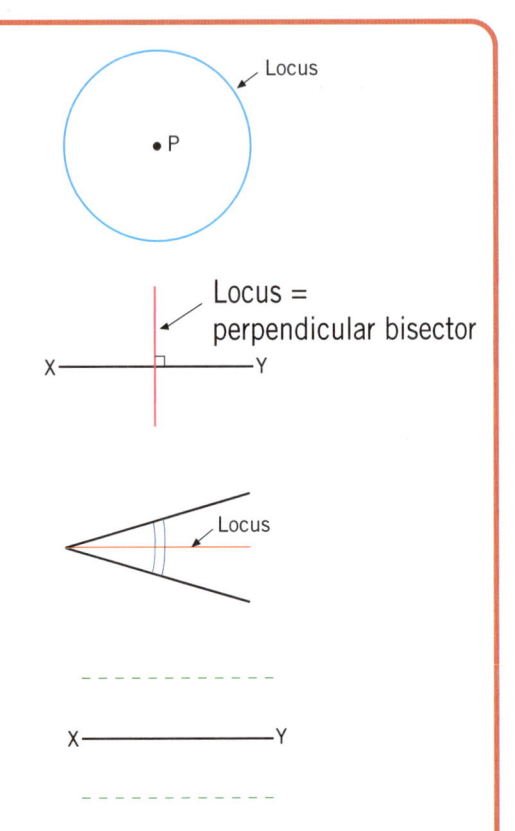

Example
A new hospital (H) is being built so that it is equidistant from the train station and the gas depot.
The hospital cannot be within 80 m of the gas depot in case of a leak.
Using a scale of 1 cm to 20 m, show the first available position for where the hospital can be built.

- Construct the perpendicular bisector of the line between the train station and the gas depot.
- With the compass point on the gas depot, draw a circle of radius 4 cm since nothing can be built within 80 m of the depot.
- The position of the hospital (H) is shown.

This diagram is not drawn to scale but is given to show you what your diagram should look like.

> When answering loci questions, measure carefully and use the construction techniques previously shown: this will ensure your work is accurate.

Coordinates

- **Coordinates** are used to locate the position of a point.

- When reading coordinates, read **across first, then up or down**.

- Coordinates are always written with **brackets**, and a **comma** in between, e.g. (2, 4).

- The horizontal axis is the *x*-axis. The vertical axis is the *y*-axis.

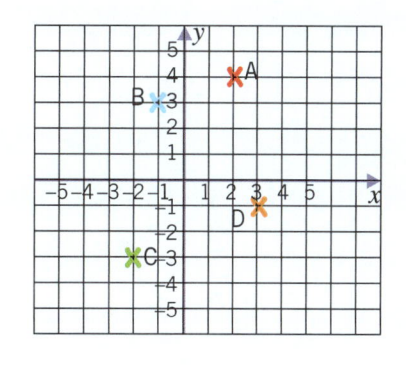

Examples
A has coordinates (2, 4)
B has coordinates (−1, 3)
C has coordinates (−2, −3)
D has coordinates (3, −1)

Coordinates in 3D

This involves the extension of the normal (*x*, *y*) coordinates into a third direction, known as *z*. All positions then have three coordinates (*x*, *y*, *z*).

Example
For the cuboid shown here the vertices of the cuboid would have the following coordinates:

O (0, 0, 0)   D (0, 2, 1)
A (3, 0, 0)   E (0, 0, 1)
B (3, 2, 0)   F (3, 0, 1)
C (0, 2, 0)   G (3, 2, 1)

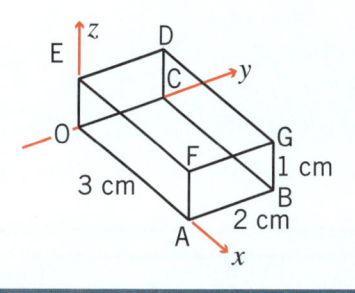

KEY TERMS

Make sure you understand these terms before moving on!
- locus
- loci
- perpendicular bisector
- coordinate
- *x*-axis
- *y*-axis

QUICK TEST

1. What are the coordinates of the points A, B, C, D, E and F?

2. A gold coin is buried in the rectangular field. It is 4 m from T and equidistant from RU and RS. Mark with an X the position of the gold coin.

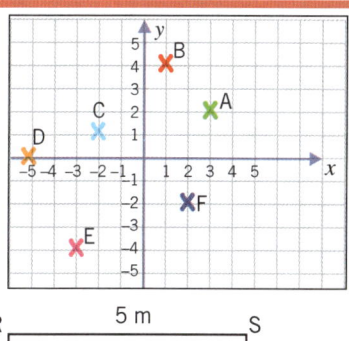

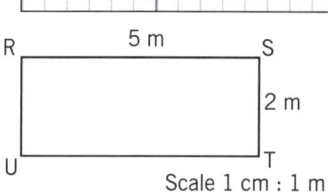

Scale 1 cm : 1 m

LOCI AND COORDINATES

Shape, space and measures

63

Pythagoras' theorem

Pythagoras' theorem states: in any right-angled triangle, the square on the *hypotenuse* is equal to the sum of the squares on the other two sides. The hypotenuse is the longest side of a right-angled triangle. It is always opposite the right angle.

Using the letters in the diagram, the theorem is written as:
$c^2 = a^2 + b^2$
This can be rearranged to give $a^2 = c^2 - b^2$ or $b^2 = c^2 - a^2$. These versions are useful when calculating the length of one of the shorter sides.

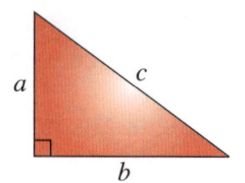

Finding the length of the hypotenuse

Remember: Pythagoras' theorem can only be used for right-angled triangles.
Step 1 Square the two numbers that you are given.
Step 2 To find the hypotenuse (the longest side), **add** these two squared numbers.
Step 3 After adding the two lengths, find the **square root** of your answer.

Example
Find the length of AB, giving your answer to 1 decimal place.
Using Pythagoras' theorem:

$(AB)^2 = (AC)^2 + (BC)^2$
$= 12^2 + 14.5^2$
$= 354.25$

So $AB = \sqrt{354.25}$ Take the square root to find AB.
$= 18.8$ m (to 1 d.p.)   Round to 1 d.p.

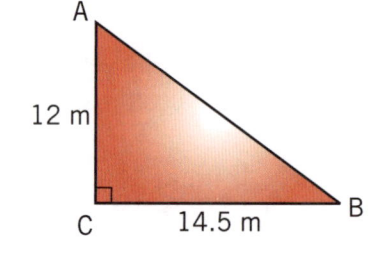

Finding the length of a shorter side

Follow the steps for finding the hypotenuse except:
Step 2 To find the shorter length, subtract the smaller value from the larger value.
- Remember to take the square root ($\sqrt{\ }$) to get your final answer.

Example
Find the length of FG, giving your answer to 1 d.p.

Using Pythagoras' theorem:

$(EF)^2 = (EG)^2 + (FG)^2$
$(FG)^2 = (EF)^2 - (EG)^2$
$= 9^2 - 8^2$
$= 81 - 64$
$= 17$
So $FG = \sqrt{17}$
$= 4.1$ cm (1 d.p.)

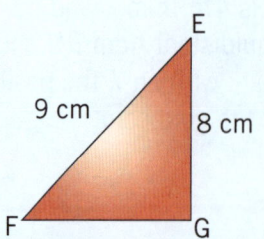

> Pythagoras' theorem allows us to calculate the length of one of the sides of a right-angled triangle, when the other two sides are known. If you are not told to what degree of accuracy to round your answer, be guided by significant figures given in the question.

Calculating the length of a line AB, given two sets of coordinates

By drawing in a triangle between the two points A (1, 2) and B (7, 6) we can use Pythagoras' Theorem to find the length of AB.

Horizontal distance = 6   (7 − 1)
Vertical distance = 4   (6 − 2)
Length of $(AB)^2 = 6^2 + 4^2$
$(AB)^2 = 36 + 16$
$(AB)^2 = 52$
$AB = \sqrt{52}$
So length of AB = 7.21

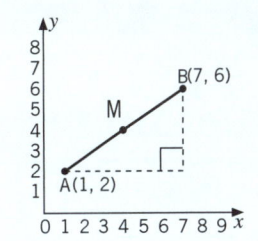

The midpoint of AB, M, has coordinates (4, 4):
$\left(\frac{1+7}{2}, \frac{2+6}{2}\right)$

Solving problems

Example
- Calculate the height of this isosceles triangle.

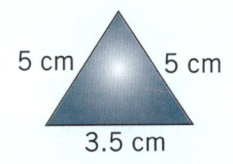

- Split the triangle down the middle to get a right-angled triangle.
Using Pythagoras' theorem:
$5^2 = h^2 + 1.75^2$
$h^2 = 5^2 - 1.75^2$
$h^2 = 21.9375$
$h = \sqrt{21.9375} = 4.68$ cm (to 2 d.p.)

Example
- A ladder of length 13 m rests against a wall. The height up the wall the ladder reaches is 12 m. How far away from the wall is the foot of the ladder?

$13^2 = x^2 + 12^2$
$x^2 = 13^2 - 12^2$
$x^2 = 169 - 144$
    = 25
So $x = \sqrt{25} = 5$ m
The foot of the ladder is 5 m away from the wall.

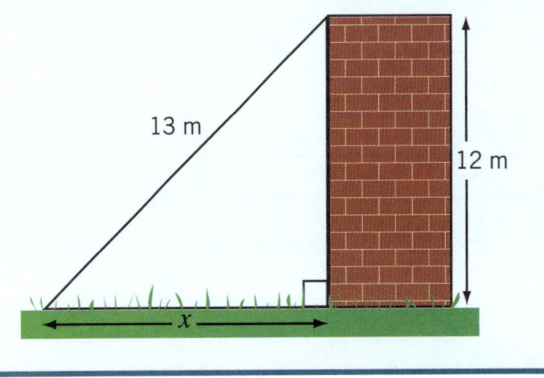

KEY TERMS
Make sure you understand these terms before moving on!
- hypotenuse
- square root

QUICK TEST

1. Calculate the lengths of the sides marked with a letter. Give your answers to 1 d.p.
   a) (triangle with x, 10.2 cm, 13.8 cm)
   b) (triangle with 15 cm, x, 25 cm)

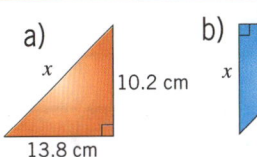

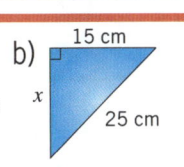

2. Work out the length of the diagonal of this rectangle. (15 cm by 8 cm)

3. A ship sets off from Port A and travels 50 km north then 80 km east to reach Port B. How far is Port A from Port B by the shortest route?

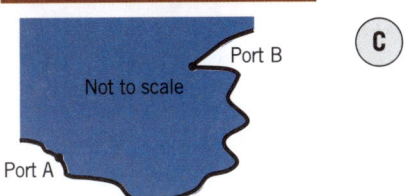

PYTHAGORAS' THEOREM

Shape, space and measures

65

Measures and measurement 1

Metric and imperial units

Metric units

Length	Weight	Capacity
10 mm = 1 cm	1000 mg = 1 g	1000 ml = 1 litre
100 cm = 1 m	1000 g = 1 kg	100 cl = 1 litre
1000 m = 1 km	1000 kg = 1 tonne	1000 cm^3 = 1 litre

Examples
500 cm = 5 m (÷ 100)
25 cm = 250 mm (× 10)
3500 g = 3.5 kg (÷ 1000)

Imperial units

Length	Weight	Capacity
1 foot = 12 inches	1 stone = 14 pounds (lb)	20 fluid oz = 1 pint
1 yard = 3 feet	1 pound = 16 ounces (oz)	8 pints = 1 gallon

Change 166 pints into gallons.
8 pints = 1 gallon, 1 pint = $\frac{1}{8}$ gallon
166 ÷ 8 = 20.75 gallons

Converting units
- If changing from **small** units **to large** units (for example, g to kg), **divide**.
- If changing from **large** units **to small** units (for example, km to m), **multiply**.

Comparisons between metric and imperial units

Length	Weight	Capacity
2.5 cm ≈ 1 inch	25 g ≈ 1 ounce	1 litre ≈ $1\frac{3}{4}$ pints
30 cm ≈ 1 foot	1 kg ≈ 2.2 pounds	4.5 litres ≈ 1 gallon
1 m ≈ 39 inches		
8 km ≈ 5 miles		

All of the comparisons between metric and imperial units are only approximate.

Example
Change 25 km into miles.

8 km ≈ 5 miles
1 km ≈ $\frac{5}{8}$ mile = 0.625 miles
25 km ≈ 25 × 0.625
= 15.625 miles

There is a lot of learning to do in this section. Try to learn all the metric and imperial conversions.

Reading scales

Decimals are usually used when reading off scales. Measuring jugs, rulers and weighing scales are all examples of scales which use decimals.

Examples

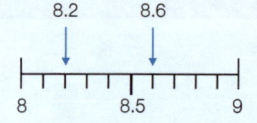

There are 10 spaces between 8 and 9. Each space represents 0.1.

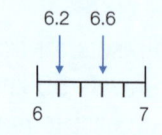

There are five spaces between 6 and 7. Each space represents 0.2.

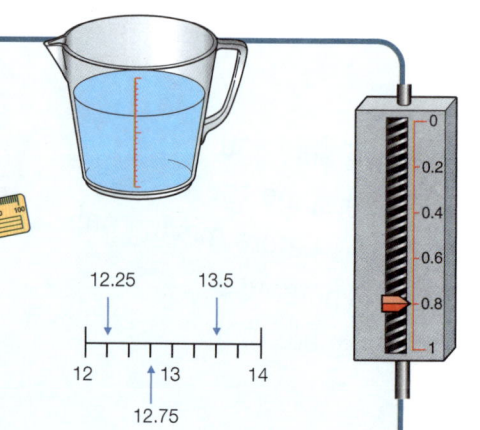

There are four spaces between 12 and 13. Each space represents 0.25.

Estimating measures

Estimates using metric and imperial units need to be made all the time.

Estimating lengths
Length and distance can be measured using two types of units.
- **Metric**: kilometres (km), metres (m), centimetres (cm) and millimetres (mm).
- **Imperial**: inches, feet, yards and miles.

Some common useful estimates:
- A door is about 2 metres high or about $6\frac{1}{2}$ feet.
- A 30 cm ruler is about 1 foot long.

Estimating capacities
Capacity is a measure of how much a container can hold.
- **Metric**: millilitres (ml), centilitres (cl), litres (l).
- **Imperial**: pints, gallons.

Some common estimates:
- A 1 pint milk carton holds about 570 ml.
- A petrol can holds 1 gallon or 4.5 litres.
- A can of pop holds about 300 ml or $\frac{1}{2}$ pint.

Estimating weights (masses)
Weight can be measured in these units:
- **Metric**: milligrams (mg), grams (g), kilograms (kg), tonnes (t).
- **Imperial**: ounces (oz), pounds (lb), stones (st), tons.

Some common estimates include:
- A 1 kg bag of sugar weighs about 2.2 lb.
- A 250 g packet of butter weighs about $\frac{1}{2}$ lb.

KEY TERMS

Make sure you understand these terms before moving on!
- metric unit
- imperial unit
- length
- weight
- capacity

QUICK TEST

1. Change 3500 g into kilograms.
2. Change 3 kg into pounds.
3. Change 6 litres into pints.
4. What do the pointers on the scales represent? 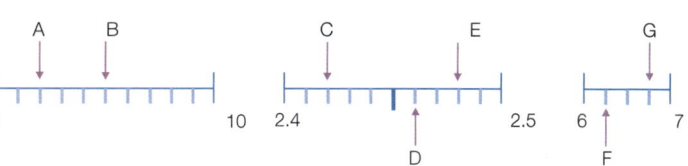
5. The weight of a newborn baby could be about:
   a) 50 g   b) 5 g   c) 3 kg   d) 30 kg

Measures and measurement 2

Timetables

Timetables often use the 24-hour clock. Timetables should be read carefully.

Example
This train timetable illustrates the train times from London to Manchester.

London, Euston	0602	0650		1100	1300
Watford Junction	0632	0720	Every 60 minutes until	1130	1330
Stoke-on-Trent	0750	0838		–	1445
Manchester, Piccadilly	0838	0926		1315	1540

There will be a train from London every 60 minutes (or 1 hour), i.e. 0750, 0850, etc.

The 0750 train from Stoke-on-Trent.

The 0650 train from London arrives in Manchester at 0926.

The 1100 from London does not stop at Stoke-on-Trent.

The 0632 train from Watford Junction takes 2 hours 6 minutes to travel to Manchester.

If the timetable is written in 24-hour clock times, make sure your answers are in 24-hour clock time.

> Reading a timetable is a very important technique to learn. You will be expected to be able to read and interpret a selection of different timetables and charts.

Accuracy of measurement

There are two types of measurements: discrete measurements and continuous measurements:
- **Discrete measures** are quantities that can be counted; for example, the number of baked bean tins on a shelf.
- **Continuous measures** are measurements which have been taken with a measuring instrument; for example, the height of a person. Continuous measures are **not exact**.

Example
Nigel weighs 72 kg to the nearest kg. His actual weight could be anywhere between 71.5 kg and 72.5 kg.

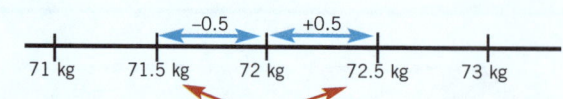

These two values are the **limits** of Nigel's weight.

If W represents Nigel's weight, then

$$71.5 \leq W < 72.5$$

This is the **lower limit** of Nigel's weight (sometimes known as the **lower bound**). Anything below 71.5 would be recorded as 71 kg.

This is the **upper limit** (**upper bound**) of Nigel's weight. Anything from 72.5 upwards would be recorded as 73 kg.

Example
The length of a seedling is measured as 3.7 cm to the nearest tenth of a cm.
What are the upper and lower limits of the length?

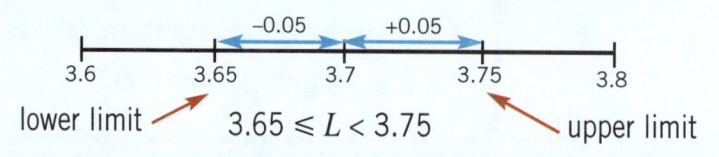

lower limit $3.65 \leq L < 3.75$ upper limit

Compound measures

Speed can be measured in kilometres per hour (km/h), miles per hour (m.p.h.) and metres per second (m/s). These are all **compound measures** because they involve a combination of basic measures.

Speed

average speed = $\dfrac{\text{total distance travelled}}{\text{total time taken}}$

$s = \dfrac{d}{t}$

Always check the units first, before starting a question. Change them if necessary.

Example
A car travels 50 miles in 1 hour 20 minutes. Find the speed in miles per hour.
Change the time units first:
20 minutes = $\dfrac{20}{60}$ of 1 hour

$s = \dfrac{d}{t} = \dfrac{50}{1\frac{20}{60}} = 37.5$ m.p.h.

From the speed formula, two other useful formulae can be found:

time = $\dfrac{\text{distance}}{\text{speed}}$ distance = speed × time

$t = \dfrac{d}{s}$ $d = st$

💡 *Just remember the letters: it's easier.*

💡 *Use the formula triangle to help you.*

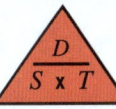

$\boxed{\dfrac{D}{S \times T}}$

Example
A car travels a distance of 240 miles at an average speed of 65 m.p.h.
How long does the journey take?

time = $\dfrac{\text{distance}}{\text{speed}}$ so $t = \dfrac{240}{65} = 3.692$ hours

3.692 hours must be changed to hours and minutes.

- Subtract the hours. So 3.692 – 3 = 0.692
- Multiply the decimal part by 60 minutes.

0.692 × 60 = 42 minutes (nearest minute)
So time = 3 hours 42 minutes

Density

density = $\dfrac{\text{mass}}{\text{volume}}$ $D = \dfrac{M}{V}$

volume = $\dfrac{\text{mass}}{\text{density}}$ mass = density × volume

$V = \dfrac{M}{D}$ $M = DV$

Example
Find the density of an object with mass 400g and volume 25 cm^3.

density = $\dfrac{M}{V} = \dfrac{400}{25} = 16$ g/cm^3

Since the mass is in grams and volume is in cm^3, density is in g/cm^3.

MEASURES AND MEASUREMENT 2

Shape, space and measures

KEY TERMS
Make sure you understand these terms before moving on!
- discrete measure
- continuous measure
- speed
- density

QUICK TEST

1. What are the upper and lower limits for a time of 9.2 seconds, rounded to the nearest tenth of a second?
2. Write down the upper and lower limits for a weight of 58 kg, rounded to the nearest kg.
3. Amy walks 6 miles in 2 hours 40 minutes. Find her average speed. **C**
4. Find the time taken for a car to travel 600 miles at an average speed of 70 m.p.h. **C**
5. Find the density of an object with mass 20 g and volume 9 cm^3. **C**

C *Indicates that a calculator may be used.*

Area of 2D shapes

Perimeter and area of 2D shapes

Perimeter: the distance around the outside edge of a shape.
Area: the amount of space a 2D shape covers. Common units of area are mm^2, cm^2, m^2, etc.

Areas of quadrilaterals and triangles

Area of a rectangle
Area = length × width $\qquad A = l \times w$

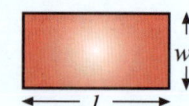

Area of a parallelogram
Area = base × perpendicular height $\qquad A = b \times h$

Remember to use the perpendicular height, not the slant height.

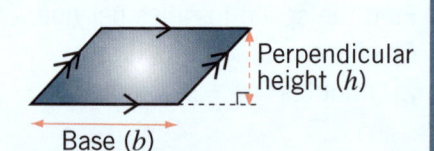

Area of a triangle
Area = ½ base × perpendicular height $\qquad A = \frac{1}{2} \times b \times h$

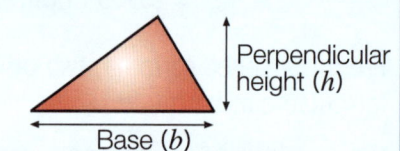

Area of a trapezium
Area = ½ × (sum of parallel sides) × perpendicular height between them

$A = \frac{1}{2}(a + b) \times h \quad$ or $\quad A = \frac{1}{2}(a + b)h$

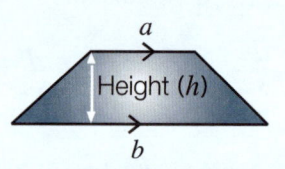

Examples
Find the areas of the following shapes, giving the answers to 3 s.f. where necessary.

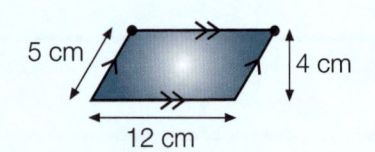

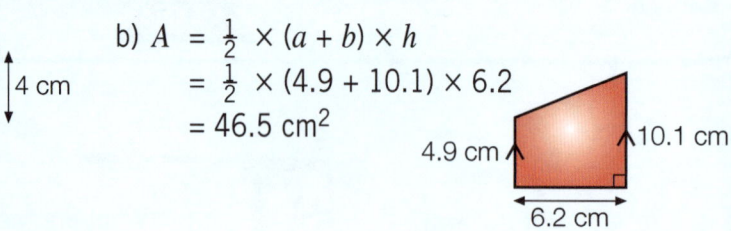

a) $A = b \times h$
$ = 12 \times 4$
$ = 48$ cm^2

b) $A = \frac{1}{2} \times (a + b) \times h$
$ = \frac{1}{2} \times (4.9 + 10.1) \times 6.2$
$ = 46.5$ cm^2

Example
If the area of this triangle is 55 cm^2, find the height, giving your answer to 3 s.f.

$A = \frac{1}{2} \times b \times h$
$55 = \frac{1}{2} \times 16.9 \times h \qquad$ Substitute the values into the formula.
$55 = 8.45 \times h \qquad\qquad$ Divide both sides by 8.45.
$h = \frac{55}{8.45}$
So $h = 6.51$ cm (to 3 s.f.)

> You have got lots more formulae to learn here. You need to know all these formulae (except the trapezium), otherwise you will find answering the questions very difficult.

Areas of enlargements and changing area units

If a shape is enlarged by a **scale factor** n then the **area** is n^2 times bigger.

Example
If $n = 2$:
- lengths are twice as big
- area is 4 times as big ($n^2 = 4$).

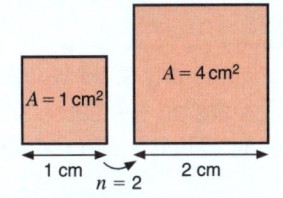

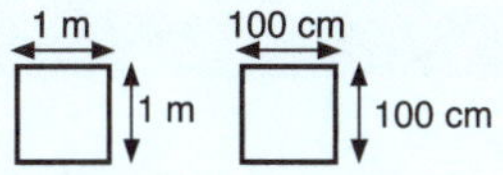

Example
The square has a length of 1 metre.
This is the same as a length of 100 cm.
Area = 1 m²   Area = 100 × 100 = 10 000 cm²
Therefore 1 m² = 10 000 cm²
(not 100 cm² as most people think!)

💡 Because of this possible mistake, it's always better to change units before you start a question.

Circumference and area of a circle

Circumference = π × **diameter** $C = \pi d$
               = π × 2 × **radius**   = $2\pi r$

Area = π × (radius)²
$A = \pi r^2$

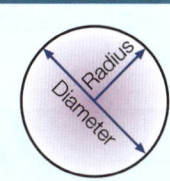

Example
The diameter of a circular rose garden is 5 m. Find the circumference and area of the garden.

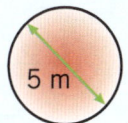

$C = \pi \times d$ Substitute in the formula.
    = 3.14 × 5   Use π = 3.14 or the value of π on your calculator.
    = 15.7 m   EXP often gives the value of π.

When finding the area, work out the radius first.
$d = 2 \times r$ so $r = d \div 2$, so $r = 2.5$ m
$A = \pi \times r^2$
    = 3.14 × 2.5²   Remember 2.5² means 2.5 × 2.5.
    = 19.625
    = 19.6 m² (3 s.f.)   This answer could be left as 6.25π, i.e. in terms of π.

Example
A circle has an area of 40 cm². Find the radius of the circle, giving your answer to 3 s.f. Use π = 3.14.

$A = \pi \times r^2$
$40 = 3.14 \times r^2$ Substitute the values into the formula.
$\frac{40}{3.14} = r^2$ Divide both sides by 3.14.
$r^2 = 12.738\ldots$
$r = \sqrt{12.738\ldots}$ Take the square root to find r.
   = 3.57 cm (3 s.f.)

KEY TERMS
Make sure you understand these terms before moving on!
- perimeter
- area
- circumference
- diameter
- radius

QUICK TEST

Work out the areas of the following shapes, giving your answers to 3 s.f.

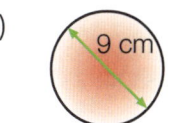

1.
   a) trapezium: 4.2 cm (top), 12.6 cm (bottom), 8.1 cm (height)
   b) parallelogram: 12 cm (base), 5.3 cm (height)
   c) circle: 9 cm (diameter)
   d) shape: 15 cm wide, 8 cm tall with semicircle top

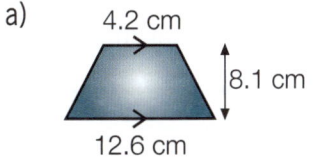

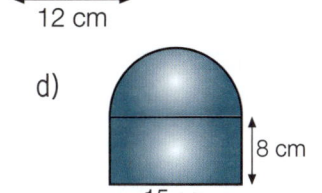

2. Work out the area of the shaded region. (10 cm × 10 cm square with circle of diameter 10 cm inside)

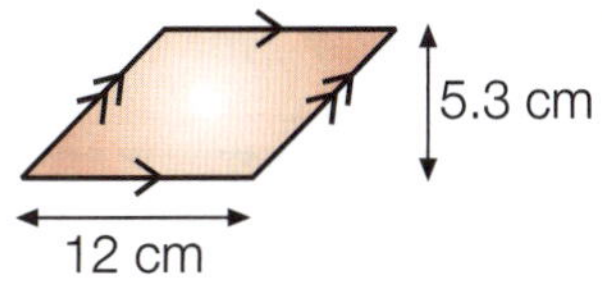

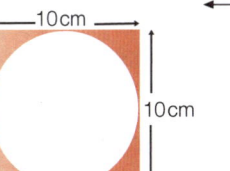

AREA OF 2D SHAPES

Shape, space and measures

71

Volume of 3D shapes

Volume is the amount of space a 3D shape occupies.
Common units of volume are mm³, cm³, m³, etc.

Volume of prisms

A **prism** is any solid which can be cut into slices, which are all the same shape.
This is called having a **uniform cross-section**.

Volume of a cuboid
volume =
length × width × height
$V = l \times w \times h$

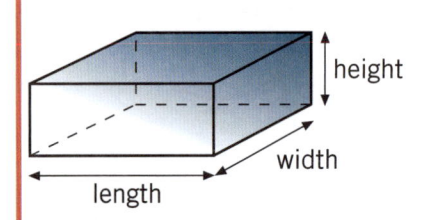

Volume of a prism
volume = area of
cross-section × length
$V = a \times l$

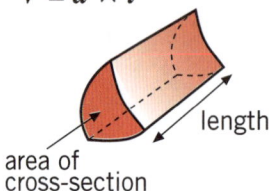

Volume of a cylinder
Cylinders are prisms where the cross-section is a circle.
volume = area of cross-section × length
$V = \pi r^2 \times h$

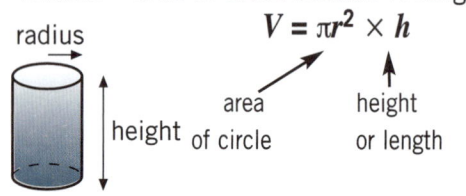

Examples
Find the volumes of the following 3D shapes, giving your answers to 3 s.f. Use π = 3.14.

a) $V = a \times l$
$= (\frac{1}{2} \times b \times h) \times l$
$= (\frac{1}{2} \times 9.6 \times 7) \times 15.1$
$= 507.36$ cm³
$= 507$ cm³ (3 s.f.)

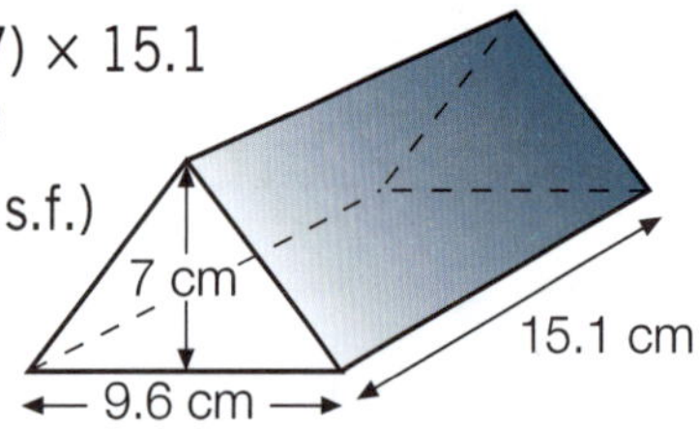

b) $V = \pi r^2 \times h$
$= 3.14 \times 10.7^2 \times 24.1$
$= 8663.92$ cm³
$= 8660$ cm³ (3 s.f.)

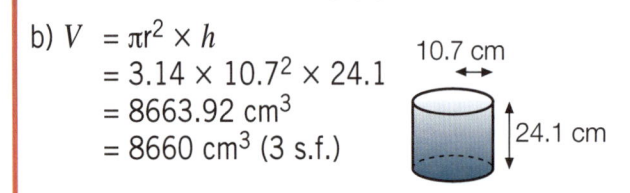

Surface area of a cylinder = $2\pi rh + 2\pi r^2$
↗ area of a rectangle
↖ area of the two circles

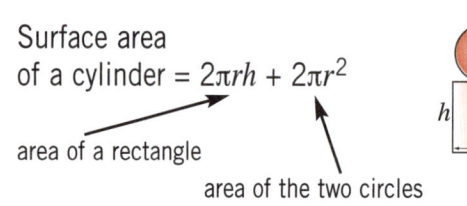

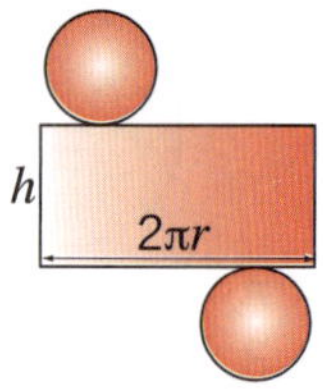

Example
Find the surface area of the following solids.
$SA = 2(hl) + 2(hw) + 2(lw)$ 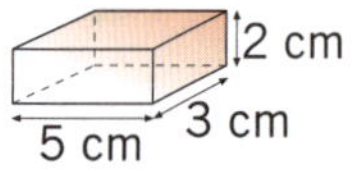
$= 2(2 \times 5) + 2(2 \times 3) + 2(5 \times 3)$
$= 2 \times (10) + 2 \times (6) + 2 \times (15)$
$= 20 + 12 + 30$
$= 62$ cm²

$SA = 2\pi rh + 2\pi r^2$
$= (2 \times \pi \times 5 \times 10) + (2 \times \pi \times 5^2)$
$= 100\pi + 50\pi$
$= 150\pi$
$= 471.2$ cm² (1 d.p.)

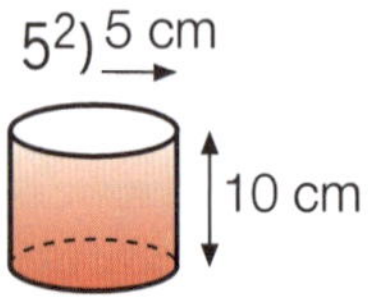

To find the surface area of a cuboid, work out the area of each face and then add them together ($SA = 2hl + 2hw + 2lw$). Surface area of a cylinder = $2\pi rh + 2\pi r^2$.

Converting volume units

Example
The cube has a length of 1 m – this is the same as a length of 100 cm.
Therefore 1 m³ = 100 × 100 × 100 = 1 000 000 cm³
Not quite what you may think!

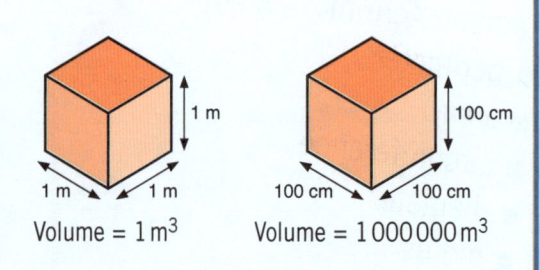

Volume = 1 m³

Volume = 1 000 000 m³

💡 *Another tricky topic which usually catches everybody out! Change all the lengths to the same unit before starting a question.*

Volumes of enlargements

For an enlargement of **scale factor n**, the volumes are n^3 **times bigger**.

Example
If a cube of length 1 cm is enlarged by a scale factor of 2:
$n = 2$, so $V = 2^3 = 8$ times bigger

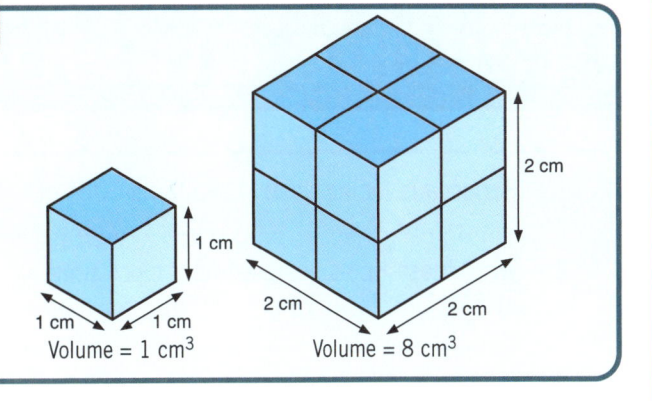

Volume = 1 cm³   Volume = 8 cm³

Dimensions

- The **dimension** of **perimeter** is **length** (L); it is a measurement in one dimension.
- The dimension of **area** is **length** × **length** ($L \times L = L^2$); it is a measurement in two dimensions.
- The dimension of **volume** is **length** × **length** × **length** ($L \times L \times L = L^3$); it is a measurement in three dimensions.
- Values like 3, $\frac{4}{\pi}$, 6.2, etc. have no dimensions.

Examples
The letters a, b, c and d all represent lengths. For each expression, write down whether it represents a length, area or volume.

a) $a^2 + b^2$ = (length × length) + (length × length) = area $L^2 + L^2$

b) $\frac{1}{3}\pi abc$ = number × length × length × length = volume L^3

c) $2\pi a + \frac{3}{4}\pi d$ = (number × length) + (number × length) = length $L + L$

d) $\frac{5}{9}\pi a^2 d + \pi b^2 c^2$ = (number × length × length × length) + (number × length² × length²) = none

$L^3 + L^4$ A dimension greater than 3 is impossible.

💡 *For any volume question, work your answer out carefully, check that you show each step in your working.*

KEY TERMS
Make sure you understand these terms before moving on!
- volume
- prism
- dimension

QUICK TEST

1. Work out the volumes of these 3D shapes. Give your answers to 3 s.f.
   a) (6.5 cm, 19.8 cm, 27.2 cm)
   b) (85 cm, 10.6 cm)

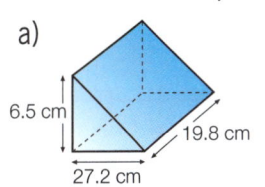

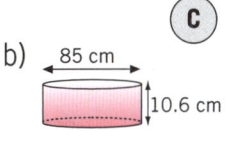

2. The volume of a cylinder is 2000 cm³ and its radius is 5.6 cm. Work out the height of the cylinder to 3 s.f.

3. x, y, z represent lengths. For each expression, write down whether it could represent perimeter, area or volume.
   a) $\sqrt{x^2 + y^2 + z^2}$
   b) $\frac{5}{9}\pi x^3 + 2y^3$
   c) $\frac{1}{3}\frac{xyz^2}{y}$
   d) $\frac{9}{5}\pi xy + \frac{4}{5}\pi yz$

Practice questions

Use the questions to test your progress.
Check your answers on page 94.

1. Rebecca is facing west. If she turns 180° clockwise, which direction will she be facing?
   ....

2. Write these times using 24-hour clock time.
   a) 7:42 am   b) 6:13 pm   c) 7:35 pm   d) 3:09 am
   ....

3. How many faces does a cuboid have?
   ....

4. Choose the correct unit from the list to complete each statement.

   | cm | kg | km | g | ml | l | m | mm |

   a) The thickness of a book is about 15 ...
   b) Gareth weighs about 65 ...
   c) A mug holds about 250 ... of water.
   ....

5. Some angles are written on cards:

   | 64° | 72° | 146° | 327° | 90° | 107° |

   Which of these angles are:
   a) acute   b) obtuse   c) reflex   d) a right angle?
   ....

6. A house plan has a scale of 1:50. If the width of the house is 42 cm on the plan, what is the real width of the house?   (C)
   ....

7. a) Draw the lines of symmetry on the rectangle.
   b) What is the order of rotational symmetry of the rectangle?

   ....

8. Calculate the sizes of the angles marked with letters.
   a ....
   b ....
   c ....
   d ....

9. Write down the readings on these scales.
   a)   b)

10. Change 600 g into pounds.
    ....

11. The scale of a road map is 1 : 25 000. Amersham and Watford are 30 cm apart on the map. Work out the real distance in km between Amersham and Watford.   (C)
    ....

(C) *Indicates that a calculator may be used.*

12. Draw the image of the shaded shape after an enlargement by scale factor ½, with C as the centre of enlargement. Label the image R.

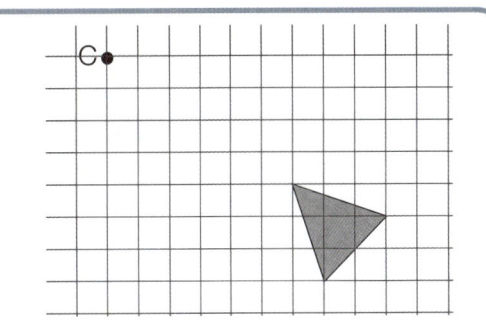

13. Work out the areas of these shapes. Give your answers to 1 decimal place.

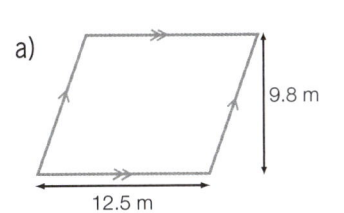

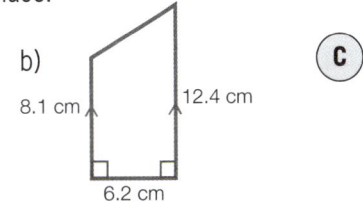

    a) 9.8 m, 12.5 m

    b) 8.1 cm, 12.4 cm, 6.2 cm

14. A car travels a distance of 320 miles at an average speed of 65 m.p.h. How long does it take?

15. A car travels 70 miles in 1 hour 20 minutes. Find the average speed in m.p.h.

16. Jerry said, 'The distance between Manchester and London is 240 miles to the nearest whole mile.' Write down the smallest possible distance between Manchester and London.

17. A ladder of length 6 m rests so that the foot of the ladder is 3 m away from a wall. Calculate how far up the wall the ladder reaches. Give your answer to 2 s.f.

18. Calculate the volume of the oil drum, clearly stating your units. Use π = 3.14. Give your answer to 3 significant figures.

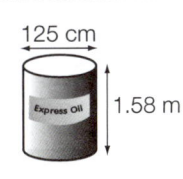

    125 cm, 1.58 m

19. Here are some expressions:

$7r^2t$	$l\sqrt{r^2+t^2}$	$\dfrac{rtl}{4}$	πr^2	$2\sqrt{r^2+t^2}$	$2tl$	$4\dfrac{r^3}{t^2}$

The letters r, t and l represent lengths. π, 2, 4 and 7 are numbers that have no dimensions. Three of the expressions represent surface area. Tick the boxes (✓) underneath these three expressions.

How well did you do? ✗ 1–5 Try again   6–10 Getting there   11–15 Good work   16–19 Excellent! ✓

Collecting data

The census is one of the largest surveys that takes place. The census is carried out every 10 years and its main aim is to give a 'snapshot' of Britain today. In order to carry out the census, all households are given a survey to complete.

Types of data

There are two main types of data:

Quantitative
the answer is a number,
e.g. how many blue cars in a car park?

Qualitative
the answer is a word,
e.g. what is your favourite colour?

Quantitative data can be discrete or continuous:

- **Discrete data** has an exact value. Each category is separate and is usually found by counting, e.g. the number of people with brown hair.
- **Continuous data** has a range of values in each category. Examples include the heights and weights of students. Continuous data cannot be measured exactly. The accuracy of the measurements relies on the accuracy of the measuring equipment.
- **Primary data** is data collected by the person who is going to analyse and use it.
- **Secondary data** is data available from an external source, such as books, newspapers and the internet.

Hypotheses and experiments

A **hypothesis** is a **prediction** which can be tested.
Experiments can be used to test hypotheses.

Example

Hypothesis: The better the light, the faster seedlings grow.

Variable: The intensity of the light – the condition that can be changed.

Conditions: The other conditions must stay the same. All seedlings must be exactly the same size, strength and colour to start with. If there is **bias** (e.g. if one side of the tray gets extra sunlight), then the experiment needs to start again.

Questionnaires

These can be used to test hypotheses.

When designing questionnaires:
- ✔ Decide what needs to be found out: the **hypothesis**.
- ✔ Give instructions on how the questionnaire has to be filled in.
- ✔ Do not ask for information which is not needed (e.g. name).
- ✔ Make the questions clear and concise.
- ✔ Keep the questionnaire short.
- ✔ If people's opinions are needed, make sure the question is **unbiased**.
  An example of a biased question:
  'Do you agree that a leisure centre should have a tennis court rather than a squash court?'
- ✔ Allow for any possible answer, for example:
  'Which of these is your favourite colour?'

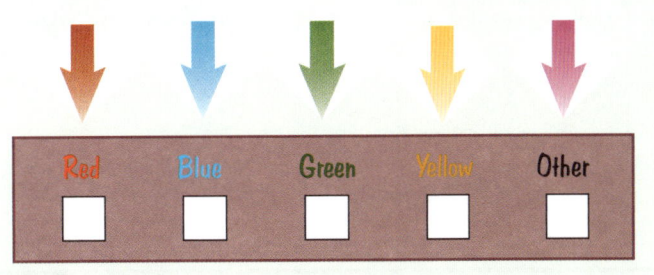

Red	Blue	Green	Yellow	Other
☐	☐	☐	☐	☐

> When asked to design a questionnaire, always word the questions carefully. Try to avoid bias appearing in your questions.

Data collection sheet

- When collecting data, a data collection sheet is often used.

Example
Tracey and David carried out a survey on the colour of cars which passed the gates of their school during a 30-minute interval. Their data collection sheet looked like this:

Colour of car	Tally	Frequency

COLLECTING DATA — Handling data

KEY TERMS

Make sure you understand these terms before moving on!
- quantitative
- qualitative
- discrete
- continuous
- hypothesis

QUICK TEST

1. Richard and Tammy are carrying out a survey to find out which are students' favourite foods.
   Design a data sheet that they could use.

2. Design a questionnaire you could give a friend in order to find out what they do in their spare time.

Representing data

Drawing pie charts

- **Pie charts** are used to illustrate data. They are circles split up into sections, each section representing a certain number of items.

Example
The favourite sports of 24 students in year 11:

Sport	Frequency	Angle	Workings
Football	9	135°	$\frac{9}{24} \times 360°$
Swimming	5	75°	$\frac{5}{24} \times 360°$
Netball	3	45°	$\frac{3}{24} \times 360°$
Hockey	7	105°	$\frac{7}{24} \times 360°$
Total	24	360°	

To calculate the angles for the pie chart:
- Find the total for the items listed.
- Find the fraction of the total for each item.
- Multiply the fraction by 360° to find the angle.

Key in on the calculator

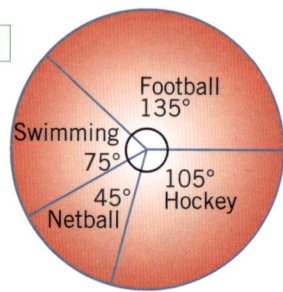

9 ÷ 24 × 360 =

Interpreting pie charts

Example
The pie chart shows how 18 students travel to school.
How many travel by a) car, b) bus and c) foot?

360° = 18 students
1° = $\frac{18}{360}$ = 0.05 (Work out what 1° represents.)

a) Car = 60 × 0.05 = 3 students
b) Bus = 80 × 0.05 = 4 students
c) Foot = 220 × 0.05 = 11 students

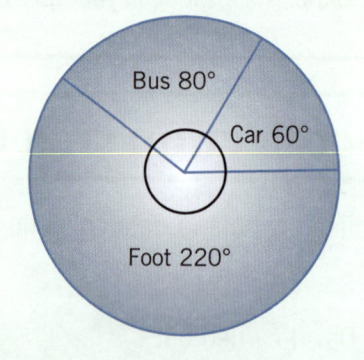

💡 Pie chart questions are usually worth about 4 marks in the GCSE exam. Check by making sure the angles add up to 360° before drawing a pie chart. Measure the angles carefully since you are allowed only a 2° tolerance.

Line graphs

- **Line graphs** are a set of points joined by lines.

Example
This example is known as a **time series** because the data was recorded at intervals of time.

Year	1988	1989	1990	1991	1992	1993
Number of cars sold	2500	2900	2100	1900	1600	800

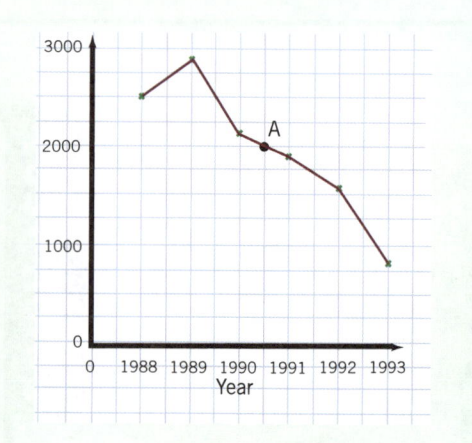

- **Middle values**, like point A, have no meaning. A does not mean that halfway between 1990 and 1991, there were 2000 cars sold.

Histograms

- Histograms are drawn to illustrate **continuous data**. They are similar to bar charts except that there are no gaps between the bars. The data must be grouped into equal **class intervals** if the length (height) of the bar is used to represent the frequency. They are also known as frequency diagrams.

Weight (kg)	Frequency
45 ≤ W < 55	7
55 ≤ W < 65	13
65 ≤ W < 75	6
75 ≤ W < 85	4

Example
The weights of 30 workers in a factory are shown in the table:

- 45 ≤ W < 55, etc, are called **class intervals** – notice they are all equal in width.
  45 ≤ W < 55 means the weights are between 45 and 55 kg.
  A weight of 55 kg would be in the next group.

Note:
- The axes do not need to start at zero.
- The axes are labelled.
- The graph has a title.

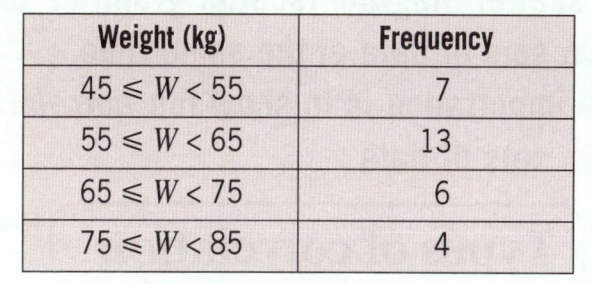

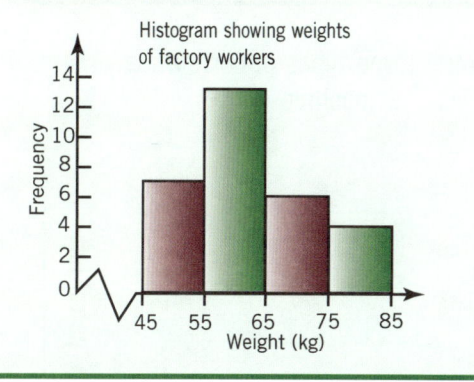

Frequency polygons

To draw a **frequency polygon**, join the **midpoints of class intervals** for grouped or continuous data.
Consider the histogram of the factory workers again.
- Put a cross on the middle of each bar and join the crosses up with a ruler.
- Draw a line down from the middle of the first and last bar to the x axis to form a closed polygon, OR
- To form an open polygon, do not join to the x axis.

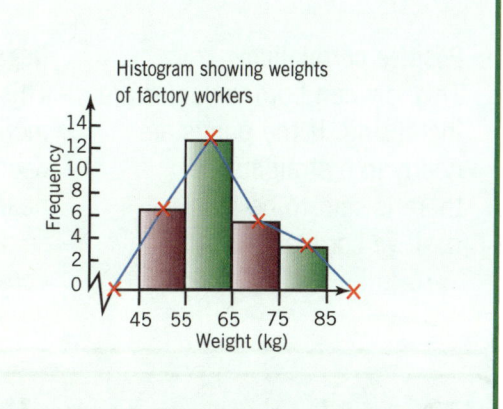

KEY TERMS

Make sure you understand these terms before moving on!
- pie chart
- line graph
- frequency polygon

QUICK TEST

1 Draw a pie chart to represent this set of data.

Hair colour	Frequency
Brown	8
Auburn	4
Blonde	6
Black	6

2 Using the histogram complete the frequency table below.

Height (h cm)	Frequency
140 ≤ h < 145	
145 ≤ h < 150	10
150 ≤ h < 155	
155 ≤ h < 160	
160 ≤ h < 165	

b) How many people were surveyed?
c) Draw a frequency polygon on the histogram.

REPRESENTING DATA — Handling data

Scatter diagrams and correlation

A scatter diagram (scatter graph or scatter plot) is used to show two sets of data at the same time.

Its importance is to show the *correlation* (connection), if any, between two sets of data.

Types of correlation

There are three types of correlation:

positive | **negative** 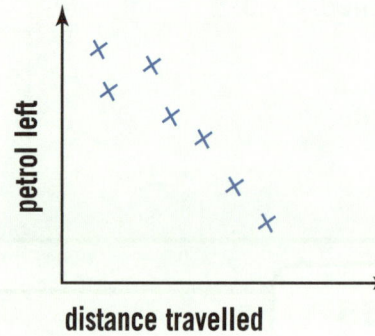 | **zero**

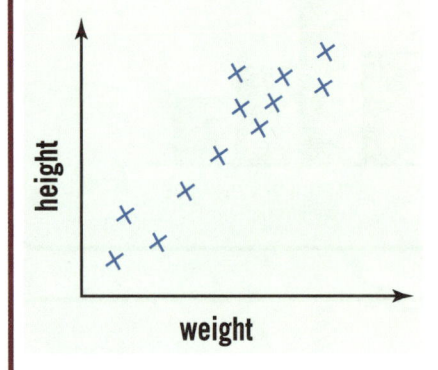

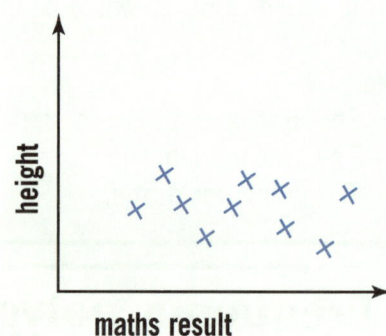

Positive correlation
This is when both variables are increasing. If the points are nearly in a straight line there is said to be high positive correlation.

Negative correlation
This is when one variable increases as the other decreases. If the points are nearly in a straight line there is said to be a high negative correlation.

Zero/no correlation
This is when there is little or no relationship between the variables.

Drawing a scatter diagram

Example
The table shows the Maths and History test results of 11 pupils.

Maths test (%)	64	79	38	42	49	75	83	82	66	61	54
History test (%)	70	36	84	70	74	42	29	33	50	56	64

The scatter diagram shows that there is a strong negative correlation – in general, the better the pupils did in Maths, the worse they did in History and vice versa.

💡 *Work out the scales first.*
Plot the points carefully.
Each time a point is plotted, tick it off your list of data.

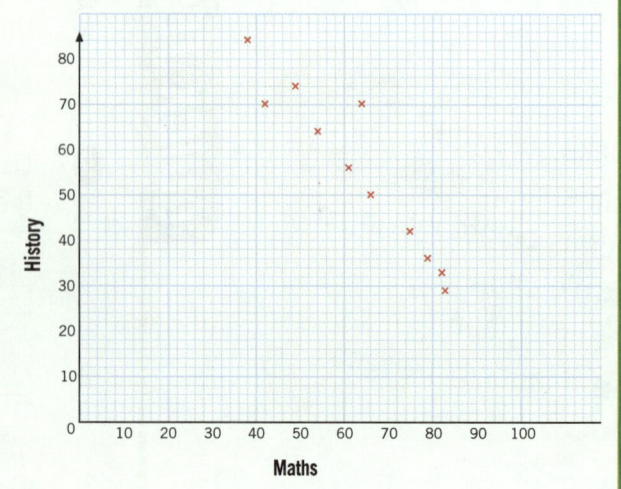

Lines of best fit

- This is the line which best fits the data points on the scatter diagram. It goes in the direction of the data and has roughly the same number of data points above the line as below it.
- A **line of best fit** can be used to make predictions.

Example

Hassam was away for a Maths test but got 78% in the History test. From the scatter diagram you can estimate he would have got approximately 43% in Maths.

Go to 78% on the History scale. Read across to the line of best fit, then down.

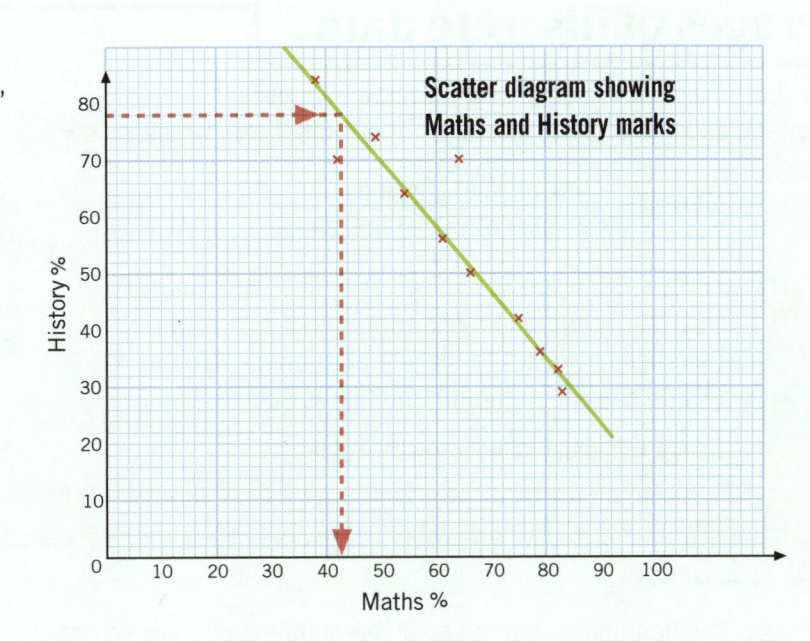

Scatter diagram showing Maths and History marks

Do not rush when drawing a scatter diagram. Plot the points very carefully. Remember to show on your graph how you made your estimates.

KEY TERMS

Make sure you understand these terms before moving on!
- correlation
- line of best fit

QUICK TEST

1. For each pair of variables, write down what type of correlation there is likely to be.
   a) Number of pages in a magazine and the number of advertisements
   b) The heights of students in a year group and the marks in their Maths test
   c) The height up a mountain and the temperature
   d) The age of a used car and its value

Averages 1

'Average height of students is 163 cm.'

Averages of discrete data

There are three types of average: **mean**, **median** and **mode**.

Mean: Sometimes known as the 'average'. The symbol for the mean is $\bar{x}$.

$$\text{Mean} = \frac{\text{sum of a set of values}}{\text{the number of values in the set}}$$

Median: The middle value when the values are put in order of size.
Mode: The value that occurs the most often in a set of data.
Range: The difference between the highest and lowest values. This tells us how much the information is spread.

$$\text{Range} = \text{highest value} - \text{lowest value}$$

Example
A football team scored the following numbers of goals in their first 10 matches:
2, 4, 0, 1, 2, 2, 3, 6, 2, 4

Find the mean, median, mode and range of the numbers of goals scored.

$$\text{Mean} = \frac{2 + 4 + 0 + 1 + 2 + 2 + 3 + 6 + 2 + 4}{10} = \frac{26}{10} = 2.6 \text{ goals}$$

Median = 0, 1, 2, 2, 2, 2, 3, 4, 4, 6   Put in order of size.

~~0~~ ~~1~~ ~~2~~ ~~2~~ (2 2) ~~3~~ ~~4~~ ~~4~~ ~~6~~   Cross off from the ends to find the middle value.

Median = $\frac{2 + 2}{2}$ = 2 goals

Mode = 2 goals   It is the most frequent score, occuring 4 times.

Range = 6 − 0 = 6   (Highest score − lowest score)

> *If there are 2 numbers in the middle of a set of values, the median is halfway between them.*

Finding a missing value when given the mean

If you are given the mean of a set of discrete data you can use the information to calculate a missing value.

Example
The mean of 15, 17, y, 28 and 19 is 16.
What is the value of y?

$$\text{Mean} = \frac{15 + 17 + y + 28 + 19}{5}$$

$$16 = \frac{79 + y}{5}$$

so $16 \times 5 = 79 + y$ This just becomes a simple equation to solve.

$80 = 79 + y$
so $y = 80 - 79$
so $y = 1$

Finding averages from a frequency table

A **frequency** table tells us how many are in a group.

Example

Number of sisters (x)	0	1	2	3	4
Frequency (f)	4	9	3	5	2

This means 2 people had 4 sisters.

Mean: $(\bar{x}) = \dfrac{\Sigma fx}{\Sigma f}$ (Σ means the **sum of**)

$= \dfrac{(4 \times 0) + (9 \times 1) + (3 \times 2) + (5 \times 3) + (2 \times 4)}{4 + 9 + 3 + 5 + 2 + 0}$

$= \dfrac{38}{23} = 1.7$ (to 1 d.p.)

Median: Since there are 23 people who have been asked the median will be the 12th person.

| 11 people | 12 | 11 people |

The 12th person has 1 sister ∴ the median = 1

Mode: This is the one with the highest frequency, that is 1 sister.

Range: 4 − 0 = 4   (Highest number of sisters − lowest)

> When finding the mean from a frequency table, remember to divide by the sum of the frequencies and not by how many groups there are.

Example

The table gives information on the number of minutes taken by a person to solve a problem.

Number of minutes (x)	0	1	2	3	4	5
Frequency (f)	1	5	6	10	3	1

Calculate the mean number of minutes taken to solve the problem.

Mean: $(\bar{x}) = \dfrac{\Sigma fx}{\Sigma f}$

$= \dfrac{(1 \times 0) + (5 \times 1) + (6 \times 2) + (10 \times 3) + (3 \times 4) + (1 \times 5)}{1 + 5 + 6 + 10 + 3 + 1}$

$= \dfrac{0 + 5 + 12 + 30 + 12 + 5}{26}$

$= \dfrac{64}{26}$

$= 2.46$ minutes (to 2 d.p.)

KEY TERMS

Make sure you understand these terms before moving on!
- mean
- median
- mode
- range
- frequency

QUICK TEST

1. Find the mean, median, mode and range of this set of data:
   2, 9, 3, 6, 4, 4, 5, 8, 4

2. Charlotte made this table to show the numbers of minutes students were late for registration one morning.

Number of minutes late (x)	0	1	2	3	4
Frequency (f)	10	4	6	3	2

   Calculate:
   a) the mean   b) the median   c) the mode   d) the range

AVERAGES 1 Handling data

Averages 2

Averages of grouped data

- When the data items are grouped into class intervals, the exact values of the data are not known.
- Estimate the mean by using the **midpoint** of the **class interval**.
- The midpoint is the halfway value.
- When using grouped (continuous) data, only the **modal class** can be found. This is the class interval with the highest frequency.

Typical GCSE question

Finding the mean of a set of grouped data is a very common GCSE question and is usually worth about 4 marks.

Example
The weights of some Year 9 pupils are shown below. Find the mean and the modal class.

Weight (kg)	Frequency (f)	Midpoint (x)	fx
$40 \leq W < 45$	7	42.5	297.5
$45 \leq W < 50$	4	47.5	190
$50 \leq W < 55$	3	52.5	157.5
$55 \leq W < 60$	1	57.5	57.5

Adding on these columns will help to show your working.

$$\text{Mean} = \frac{\Sigma fx}{\Sigma f} = \frac{(7 \times 42.5) + (4 \times 47.5) + (3 \times 52.5) + (1 \times 57.5)}{7 + 4 + 3 + 1}$$

$$= \frac{702.5}{15}$$

$$= 46.8 \text{ kg (1 d.p.)}$$

Modal class = $40 \leq W < 45$

This is the same sort of question as you saw on page 83, except the frequency is multiplied by the **midpoint** of each class interval.

If your calculator will do statistical calculations learn how to use these functions. It is much quicker, but always do it twice as a check. Always show full working out still in order to obtain some method marks.

Using appropriate averages

- The **mean** is useful when a 'typical' value is wanted. Be careful not to use the mean if there are extreme values.
- The **median** is a useful average to use if there are extreme values.
- The **mode** is useful when the most common value is needed.

Stem and leaf diagrams

Stem and leaf diagrams are another way of recording information and they can also be used to find the mode, median and range of a set of data.

Example
Here are some marks gained by some students in a mathematics exam:
24 61 55 36 42
32 60 51 38 58
55 52 47 55 55

Stem is 30, leaf is 2 ∴ 32

When the information is put into a stem and leaf diagram, it looks like this:

```
stem | leaf
  2  | 4
  3  | 2 6 8
  4  | 2 7
  5  | 1 2 5 5 5 5 8
  6  | 0 1
```

Stem = 10 marks
To read off the values, you multiply the stem by 10 and add on the leaf. Using the stem and leaf the mode, median and range can be found easily:
mode   = 55
median   = 52
range   = 61 – 24 = 37

Stem and leaf diagrams are useful when comparing two sets of data.

Using averages and spread to compare distributions

Be careful when drawing conclusions from averages, as they do not always tell the whole story.

Example
11A obtained a mean of 57% in a test and the range was 79.
11T obtained a mean of 84% in the same test and their range was 18.

From the averages we would say that 11T is better than 11A. However, look at the ranges for each class:
11A = 100% – 21% = 79%
11T = 94% – 76% = 18%

Using the ranges, it can be seen that not all of 11T are better than 11A; some of 11A obtained higher marks than anyone in 11T. The average of 11A has been lowered because of the low marks obtained by some pupils.

AVERAGES 2 — Handling data

KEY TERMS

Make sure you understand these terms before moving on!
- modal class
- stem and leaf diagram

QUICK TEST

1 The heights of some Year 10 pupils are shown in the table: **C**

Height	Frequency
$140 \leqslant h < 145$	4
$145 \leqslant h < 150$	7
$150 \leqslant h < 155$	14
$155 \leqslant h < 160$	5
$160 \leqslant h < 165$	2

a) Calculate an estimate for the mean of this data.
b) Write down the modal class.

Probability 1

Probability is the chance or likelihood that something will happen. All probabilities lie between 0 and 1 inclusive.

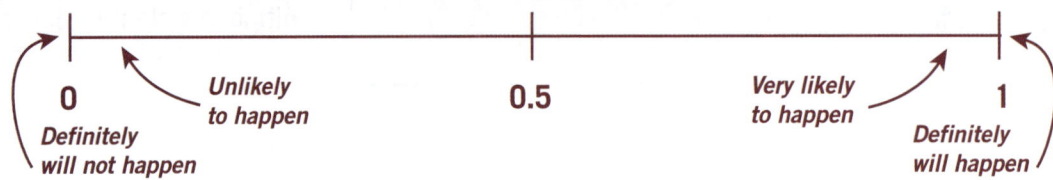

```
0 ———————————————— 0.5 ———————————————— 1
Definitely    Unlikely              Very likely    Definitely
will not      to happen             to happen      will happen
happen
```

What is probability?

Exhaustive events account for all possible outcomes.
For example, the list HH, HT, TH, TT gives all possible outcomes when two coins are thrown simultaneously.

Mutually exclusive events or outcomes cannot happen at the same time.
For example, if a student is chosen at random:

Event A: the student is a girl } These are **mutually exclusive** because no
Event B: the student is a boy   } student can be both a boy and a girl.

Event C: the student has brown hair } These are **not mutually exclusive** because
Event D: the student wears glasses   } brown-haired students can wear glasses.

Probability of an outcome = $\dfrac{\text{number of ways an outcome can happen}}{\text{total number of outcomes}}$

P(event) is a shortened way of writing 'probability of an event'.

> Probabilities can be written as a fraction, decimal or percentage. Probabilities can never be greater than 1.

Example
There are 6 blue, 4 yellow and 2 red beads in a bag.
John chooses a bead at random. What is the probability he chooses:

a) a red bead?
b) a yellow bead?
c) a blue, yellow or red bead?
d) a white bead?

a) P(red) = $\frac{2}{12}$ or $\frac{1}{6}$
b) P(yellow) = $\frac{4}{12}$ or $\frac{1}{3}$
c) P(blue, yellow or red) = $\frac{12}{12}$ = 1
d) P(white) = 0

Expected number

Example
If a fair die is thrown 300 times, approximately how many fives are likely to be obtained?
There are six possible outcomes and all are equally likely.

P(5) = $\frac{1}{6}$ × 300 = 50 fives

Multiply 300 by $\frac{1}{6}$ since a 5 is expected $\frac{1}{6}$ of the time.

Example
The probability of passing a driving test at the first attempt is 0.65. If there are 200 people taking their test for the first time, how many would you expect to pass the test?

0.65 × 200 = 130 people

Relative frequencies

Relative frequencies can be used as an estimate of probability.
If it is not possible to calculate probability, an experiment is used to find the relative frequency.

$$\text{Relative frequency of an event} = \frac{\text{number of times event occurred}}{\text{total number of trials}}$$

Example
When a fair die was thrown 80 times, a six came up 12 times.
What is the relative frequency of getting a six?

number of trials = 80   number of sixes = 12
relative frequency = $\frac{12}{80}$ = 0.15

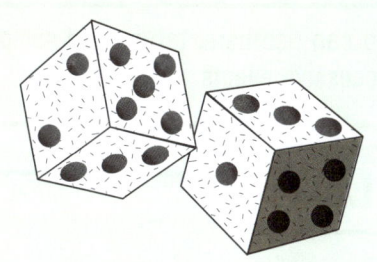

Using experiments to calculate relative frequencies

If a die is thrown 180 times it would be expected that 30 twos would be thrown.
$\frac{1}{6} \times 180 = 30$

Example
Throw the die 180 times and record the frequency of twos in every 30 throws.

Number of throws	Total frequency of twos	Relative frequency
30	3	0.1
60	7	0.12
90	16	0.18
120	19	0.16
150	24	0.16
180	31	0.17

The relative frequency is obtained by dividing the total frequency of twos by number of throws, i.e. $\frac{16}{90}$.

It is expected that one-sixth ($\frac{1}{6} = 0.16\dot{6} = 0.17$) of the throws will be twos.
As the number of throws increases, the relative frequency gets closer to the expected probability.

KEY TERMS

Make sure you understand these terms before moving on!
- probability
- exhaustive events

QUICK TEST

1. Write down an event that will have a probability of zero.

2. A box contains 3 salt 'n' vinegar, 4 cheese and 2 bacon flavoured packets of crisps. If a packet of crisps is chosen at random, what is the probability that the flavour is:
   a) salt 'n' vinegar?   b) cheese?   c) onion?

3. The probability of achieving a grade C in Maths is 0.48. If 500 students sit the exam, how many would you expect to achieve a grade C?

4. When a fair die was thrown 200 times, a five came up 47 times. What is the relative frequency of getting a five?

Probability 2

Possible outcomes of two or more events

You can use lists, tables and **sample space diagrams** when answering probability questions with two **successive events**.

Lists

Making a systematic list of possible outcomes of two events is useful.

Example
A coin is thrown twice. Make a list of the possible outcomes.
What is the probability of getting two heads?

There are four different outcomes:

HH	TT	HT	TH
both heads	both tails	1st head, 2nd tail	1st tail, 2nd head

$P(HH) = \frac{1}{4}$

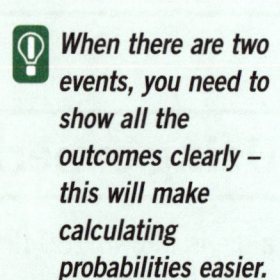

> When there are two events, you need to show all the outcomes clearly – this will make calculating probabilities easier.

Sample space diagrams

A table is helpful when considering outcomes of two events. This kind of table is sometimes known as a **sample space diagram**.

Example
Two dice are thrown together and their scores are added. Draw a diagram to show all the outcomes.
Find the probability of:
a) a score of 7.
b) a score that is a multiple of 4.

a) $P(\text{score of 7}) = \frac{6}{36} = \frac{1}{6}$
b) $P(\text{multiple of 4}) = \frac{9}{36} = \frac{1}{4}$

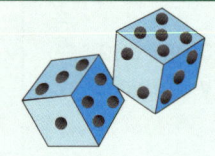

		First die					
		1	2	3	4	5	6
Second die	1	2	3	4	5	6	7
	2	3	4	5	6	7	8
	3	4	5	6	7	8	9
	4	5	6	7	8	9	10
	5	6	7	8	9	10	11
	6	7	8	9	10	11	12

There are 36 possible outcomes.

Two-way tables

Example
The **two-way table** shows the number of students in a class who are left-handed or right-handed.

Hand	Male	Female	Total
Right	14	10	24
Left	2	7	9
Total	16	17	33

a) What is the probability that a person chosen at random is right-handed?

$P(\text{right-handed}) = \frac{24}{33} = \frac{8}{11}$

b) If a boy is chosen at random, what is the probability that he is left-handed?

$P(\text{left-handed boy}) = \frac{2}{16} = \frac{1}{8}$

Probability of an event not happening

If two events are **mutually exclusive**, then:

P (event will happen) = 1 − P (event will not happen)
or
P (event will not happen) = 1 − P (event will happen)

Example
The probability that someone will get flu next winter is 0.42.
What is the probability that they won't get flu next winter?

P (not get flu) = 1 − P (get flu)
= 1 − 0.42
= 0.58

Example
Mrs Smith chooses one book from her library each week. She chooses a horror story, a thriller or a crime novel.

The probability that she chooses a horror story is 0.35.
The probability that she chooses a thriller is 0.25.

Work out the probability that Mrs Smith chooses a crime novel.

Probability she chooses a horror story or thriller is 0.35 + 0.25 = 0.6

Probability she chooses a crime novel is

1 − P (does not choose a crime novel)
= 1 − 0.6
= 0.4

The addition law

If two or more events are **mutually exclusive** the probability of A or B or C . . . happening is found by **adding** the probabilities.
P (A or B or C. . .) = P(A) + P(B) + P(C) + . . .

Example
There are 11 counters in a bag: 5 of the counters are red and 3 of them are white. Lucy picks a counter at random. Find the probability that Lucy's counter is either red or white.

$P(red) = \frac{5}{11}$ $P(white) = \frac{3}{11}$

P(red or white) = P(red) + P(white)

$\frac{5}{11} + \frac{3}{11} = \frac{8}{11}$ Red and white are mutually exclusive

PROBABILITY 2 Handling data

KEY TERMS
Make sure you understand these terms before moving on!
- sample space diagram
- two-way table

QUICK TEST

1. The probability that it will not rain tomorrow is $\frac{2}{9}$. What is the probability that it *will* rain tomorrow?

2. a) Draw a sample space diagram which shows the possible outcomes when two dice are thrown together and their scores are multiplied.
   b) What is the probability of a score of 6?
   c) What is the probability of a score of 37?

Practice questions

Use the questions to test your progress.
Check your answers on page 95.

1. The number of mm of rainfall that fell during the first eight days of August are shown in the table below.
   a) Draw a line graph to display this information
   b) Work out the mean monthly rainfall for the first eight days of August.

Day	1	2	3	4	5	6	7	8
Rainfall (mm)	12	4	7	2	5	1	2	6

2. Reece carried out a survey to find out the favourite flavours of crisps of students in his class. The results are shown in the table (right). Draw a pie chart of this information.

Crisp flavour	Number of students
Cheese and onion	7
Salt and vinegar	10
Beef	6
Smokey bacon	1

3. Find the mean, median and mode of these quantities: 6, 2, 1, 4, 2, 2, 5, 3

4. A bag contains three red, four blue and six green balls. If a ball is chosen at random from the bag, what is the probability of choosing:
   a) a red ball   b) a green ball   c) a yellow ball   d) a blue or red ball?

5. The probablility that Josie gets full marks in a tables test is 0.82. What is the probablility that she does not get full marks in a tables test?

6. A youth club has 75 members, of which 42 are boys.
   There are 15 members who are boys under 13 years old.
   There are 21 members who are girls over 13 years old.
   a) Complete the two way table.
   b) How many of the girls are under 13 years old?

	Under 13 years old	13 years old and over	Totals
Boys			
Girls			
Total			

7. The pie chart below shows how Erin spends a typical day.
   a) Measure the size of the angle for sleeping. ....
   b) Work out the number of hours that Erin works. ....
   c) For how many hours does Erin watch TV? ....

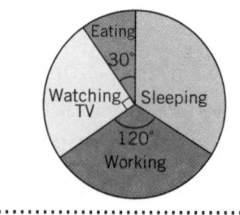

8. The probablity of passing a driving test is 0.7.
   If 200 people take the test today, how many would you expect to pass?

9. Michelle is a swimmer. The probability of her winning a race is 84%. If she swims in 50 races this season, how many races would you expect her to win?

10. A die is thrown and the scores are noted. The results are shown in this table: **C**
    Work out the mean die score.

Die score	1	2	3	4	5	6
Frequency	12	15	10	8	14	13

C Indicates that a calculator may be used.

11. In a survey the heights of ten girls and their shoe sizes were measured:

Height in cm	150	157	159	161	158	164	154	152	162	168
Shoe size	3	5	$5\frac{1}{2}$	6	5	$6\frac{1}{2}$	4	$3\frac{1}{2}$	6	7

   a) Draw a scatter diagram to illustrate this data.
   b) What type of correlation is there between height and shoe size? ....
   c) Draw a line of best fit on your diagram. ....
   d) From your scatter diagram, estimate the height of a girl whose shoe size is $4\frac{1}{2}$. ....
   ....

12. Two spinners are used in a game. The first spinner is labelled 2, 4, 6, 8.
    The second spinner is labelled 3, 5, 5, 7. Both spinners are spun.
    The score is found by multiplying the numbers on each spinner.

		First spinner			
		2	4	6	8
Second spinner	3				
	5				
	5				
	7				

    a) Complete the table to show the possible scores:
    b) What is the probability of getting an even score? ....
    c) What is the probability of getting a score of 10? ....
    ....

13. The weights of some students in a class are measured.
    The results are given in the table.

Weight in kg	Number of students
$40 \leq W < 45$	6
$45 \leq W < 50$	5
$50 \leq W < 55$	8
$55 \leq W < 60$	4
$60 \leq W < 65$	2

    a) Work out an estimate for the mean weight of the students.
    ....

    b) What is the modal class? ....
    ....

14. The daily number of guests in a hotel over a two-week period was recorded.

    42 38 27 52 37 56 25
    57 28 44 50 39 38 46

    a) Complete the stem-and-leaf diagram. Use the tens digit as the stem.

    Number of guests

Stem	Leaf
2	
3	
4	
5	

    Key 3|6 means 36

    b) Use the diagram to find:

    (i) the mode ....

    (ii) the range. ....

Answers

Number
Quick test answers

Page 5 Numbers
1. 2, 3, 5, 7, 11, 13, 17, 19
2. HCF: 12; LCM: 120
3. a) ±8 b) 6
4. a) $\frac{12}{9}$ b) $\frac{p}{x}$

Page 7 Positive and negative numbers
1. 3°C
2. a) 4 b) –16 c) –12 d) –12 e) 5 f) 6 g) 7 h) –10 i) 36

Page 9 Working with numbers
1. a) 1177 b) 232 c) 1722 d) 275
2. 20 496
3. 37
4. a) 164 b) 890 c) 37 000 d) 0.097
5. 42 people

Page 11 Fractions
1. a) $\frac{1}{3}$ b) $\frac{7}{20}$ c) $\frac{6}{13}$ d) $1\frac{1}{3}$ e) $\frac{5}{21}$ f) $\frac{4}{21}$ g) $\frac{49}{121}$ h) $\frac{50}{63}$
2. £40
3. 247 mm

Page 13 Decimals
1. a) 36.48 b) 17.679 c) 26.88 d) 12.3 e) 6 f) 52 g) 0.4 h) 0.0037 i) 4000 j) 45 000 k) 470 000 l) 32 500
2. a) 2.607, 2.61, 2.615, 4.02, 4.021, 4.20 b) 6.05, 6.49, 8.206, 8.27, 8.271, 8.93
3. a) 693 b) 291 c) 7.074 d) 0.0284 e) 7650 f) 0.2719

Page 15 Rounding
1. a) 30 b) 2740 c) 1050 d) 32 770
2. a) 6.43 b) 18.61 c) 14.27 d) 29.64
3. a) 2800 b) 270 c) 39 000 d) 0.027

Page 17 Percentages 1
1. £210   2. 74.6%   3. 9.9 lb   4. Super's; £33.33

Page 19 Percentages 2
1. £289   2. a) £1800 b) £6180   3. £100 440   4. £3394.88

Page 20 Equivalents
1. i) a) 0.2857 b) 28.57% (2 d.p.) ii) a) 0.6 b) 60% iii) a) $0.8\dot{8}$ b) $88.8\dot{8}$%
2. 0.041, 5%, 26%, $\frac{1}{3}$, $\frac{2}{5}$, 0.42

Page 21 Using a calculator
a) 14.45 (2 d.p.) b) 769.6 (1 d.p.) c) 7.052 (3 d.p.) d) $8\frac{1}{3}$ or $8.\dot{3}$

Page 23 Approximating and checking calculations
1. 100   2. 10 rolls of wallpaper   3. £4.75

Page 25 Ratio
1. a) 4 : 5 b) 1 : 2 c) 5 : 2
2. 10, 15 and 35 sweets, respectively
3. £2.76   4. 36 cm

Page 27 Indices
1. a) 12^{12} b) 9^6 c) 4 d) 18^8 e) 4^5 f) 1
2. a) x^{13} b) $6x^{16}$ c) $4x^2$ d) $5x^{11}$ e) $2x^{12}$

Page 28–29 Answers to practice questions
1. a) 9, 21, 41 b) 9, 64, 100 c) 2, 41 d) 2, 40 e) 40, 64, 100
2. 9°
3. a) 44 764 b) 27
4. a) 56 b) 508 c) 7002
5. six million, four hundred and fifty-seven thousand, two hundred and seventy-nine
6. 27, 405, 639, 728, 736, 829
7. 8 boxes
8. 77.3%
9. £315
10. 5.032, 5.04, 5.42, 6.27, 6.385, 6.39
11. 4 : 5
12. 750 g self raising flour, 375 g butter, 625 g sugar, 5 eggs
13. £25 000
14. a) 365 b) 0.706
15. $\frac{9+9}{0.2 \times 50} = \frac{18}{10} = 1.8$
16. The 100 ml tube of toothpaste
17. 1.5 cm
18. £6502.50
19. £715.02
20. 20%
21. a) $2^3 \times 3^2 = 8 \times 9 = 72$
    b) a^7
    c) b^4
    d) $\frac{16a^9}{4a^2} = 4a^7$

Algebra
Quick test answers

Page 31 Algebra 1
1. a) $10a$ b) $8a + b$ c) $9x + 4y$ d) $4x^2y - 5xy^2$
2. a) –19.2 b) 28.8 c) 0.94 d) 53.8

Page 33 Algebra 2
1. a) $3x + 6$ b) $2x + 2y$ c) $-6x - 12$ d) $x^2 + 5x + 6$ e) $y^2 - 7y + 12$ f) $a^2 + 4a + 4$
2. a) $6(x - 3)$ b) $5(y - 3)$ c) $5(a + 4)$ d) $10x(2x + 1)$ e) $5y(3 - 4y)$ f) $20xy(x + 2)$
3. $b = \frac{a + d}{5}$
4. $m = \frac{y - c}{x}$

Page 35 Equations 1
1. $x = 4$ 2. $x = 6$ 3. $x = 20$ 4. $x = 13$ 5. $x = 24$ 6. $x = 4.5$
7. $x = 2$ 8. $x = 4$ 9. $x = -1$ 10. $x = -1.4$

Page 37 Equations 2
1. $x = 3, y = -1$
2. 3.3
3. a) $4(x + 1)$ cm $= 4x + 4$ cm b) $x = 9$ ∴ length $= 11$ cm

Page 39 Patterns, sequences and inequalities
1. a) 13, 15 b) 25, 36 c) 4, 2
2. a) $2n + 3$ b) $3n - 1$ c) $4n + 2$ d) $10 - 2n$
3. a) $x < 6$ b) $x \geq 4$ c) $1 \leq x \leq 3$ d) $-\frac{1}{5} \leq x < 2$

Page 41 Straight line graphs

1. a) $x = 1$ b) $x = 1.5$
2. a) Gradient 2; Intercept (0, 4); b) Gradient 3; Intercept (0, –2)
   c) Gradient 3; Intercept (0, 2)

Page 43 Curved graphs

1. a)

x	–3	–2	–1	0	1	2	3
y	12	7	4	3	4	7	12

b) [graph of $y = x^2 + 3$]

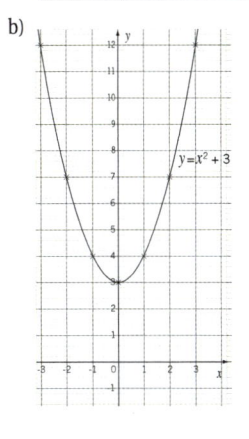

c) $x = 2.2$ and $–2.2$ aproximately

2. a)

x	–3	–2	–1	0	1	2	3
y	17	7	1	–1	1	7	17

2. b) [graph of $y = 2x^2 - 1$]

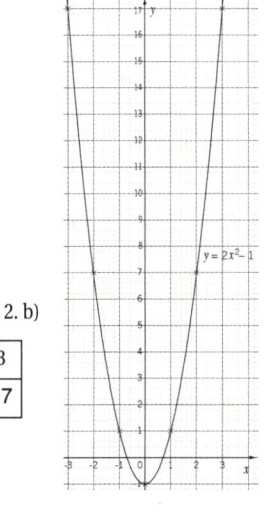

Page 45 Interpreting graphs

1. Container A – graph 3 Container B – graph 1 Container C – graph 2
2. a) $66.\dot{6}$ m.p.h. b) 1 hour c) 50 m.p.h. d) About 1442

Page 46–47 Answers to practice questions

1. $T = 85y + 8z$
2. a) [matchstick pattern]

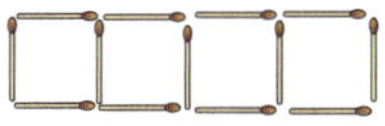

b)

Pattern number	Number of matchsticks
1	4
2	7
3	10
4	13
5	16
6	19

c) 301 matchsticks d) $m = 3p + 1$

3. a) $n = 7$ b) $n = 14$ c) $n = 7$ d) $n = 18$
4. a) $5n + 10$ b) $3n – 6$ c) $2n – 10$ d) $–3n + 18$
5. 21, 25
6. a) $x = 3$ b) $x = 4$ c) $x = 5$ d) $x = 2$ e) $x = 1$
7. a) $9x + 4 = 22$ b) 3 cm

8. a)

x	–2	–1	0	1	2	3
$y = 3x – 4$	–10	–7	–4	–1	2	5

b) [graph of $y = 3x - 4$]

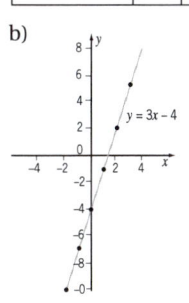

c) $(\frac{4}{3}, 0)$

9. $2n^2 + 1$
10. a) $4a$ b) $5b$ c) $3b$ d) $6c$ e) $8a – b$
11. a) $5(a – 2)$ b) $6(b + 2)$ c) $4y(2y + 3)$
12. a) x^7 b) b^3 c) $12x^5$
13. a) 3 b) 10
14. $P = 54.3$ (3 s.f.) b) $y = \dfrac{P^2 + 3x^2}{5x}$
15. $x = 1.8$ (1 d.p.)
16. $1 \leq n \leq 3$
17. Graph 1 = C Graph 2 = A Graph 3 = B
18. $4n – 1$

Shape, space and measure
Quick test answers

Page 49 Shapes

1. Hexagon 2. See information on pages 48/9.

Page 51 Solids

1. [net of solid with 4 cm and 5.7 cm measurements]

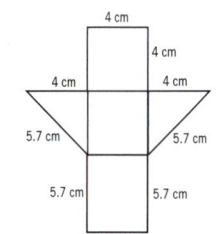

2. [views: view from A (front elevation), side elevation B, plan]

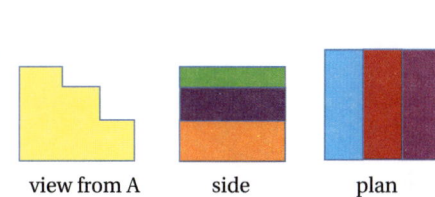

Page 52 Symmetry

1. Plane, rotational, reflective
2. [symmetry diagram]
3. [house-shaped prism with plane of symmetry]

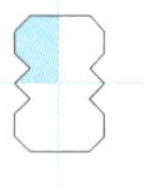

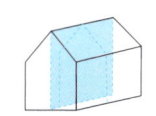

Page 53 Constructions

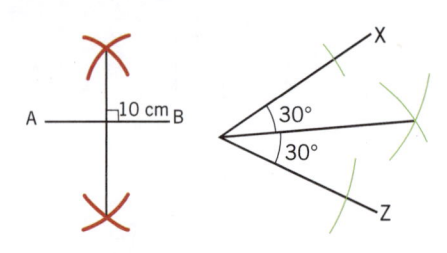

Page 55 Angles

1. a) $a = 150°$ b) $b = 70°$, $c = 110°$, $d = 70°$ c) $a = 50°$, $b = 50°$, $c = 130°$, $d = 50°$

2. a) 72° b) 108°

Page 57 Bearings and scale drawings

1. a) 072° b) 305° c) 145°

2. a) 252° b) 125° c) 325° 3. 7 km

Page 59 Transformations 1

1.

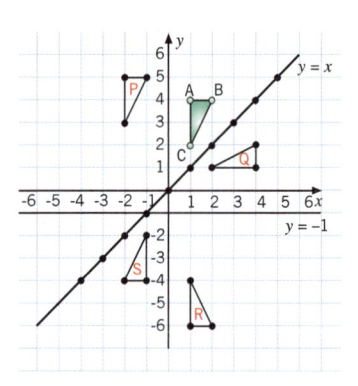

2. Move 2 to the left, 3 upwards

Page 61 Transformations 2

1.

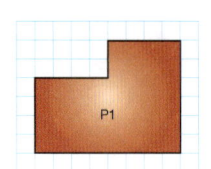

2.

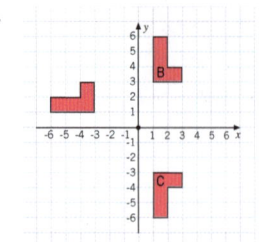

Page 63 Loci and coordinates

1. A(3, 2), B(1, 4), C(–2, 1), D(–5, 0), E(–3, –4), F(2, –2)

2.

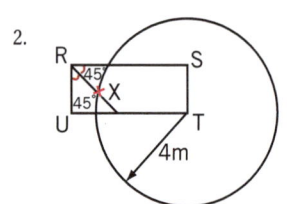

Page 65 Pythagoras' theorem

1. a) 17.2 cm b) 20.0 cm 2. 17 cm 3. 94.3 km

Page 67 Measures and measurement 1

1. 3.5 kg
2. 6.6 lb
3. $10\frac{1}{2}$ pints
4. A = 9.2, B = 9.5, C = 2.42, D = 2.46, E = 2.48, F = 6.25, G = 6.75
5. c) 3 kg

Page 69 Measures and measurement 2

1. $9.15 \leq t < 9.25$
2. $57.5 \leq W < 58.5$
3. 2.25 m.p.h.
4. 8.57 hours (or 8 hours 34 minutes)
5. 2.2 g/cm^3

Page 71 Area of 2D shapes

1. a) 68.0 cm^2 (3 s.f.) b) 63.6 cm^2 (3 s.f.) c) 63.6 cm^2 (3 s.f.)
   d) 208 cm^2 (3 s.f.) 2. 21.5 cm^2 (3 s.f.)

Page 73 Volume of 3D shapes

1. a) 1750 cm^3 (3 s.f.) b) 60 100 cm^3 (3 s.f.)
2. 20.3 cm (3 s.f.)
3. a) Perimeter b) Volume c) Volume d) Area

Page 74–75 Answers to practice questions

1. East
2. a) 0742 b) 1813 c) 1935 d) 0309
3. 6 faces
4. a) mm b) kg c) ml
5. a) 64°, 72° b) 146°, 107° c) 327° d) 90°
6. 21 m
7. a) 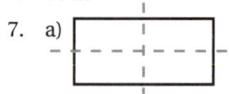 b) Order 2
8. $a = 80°$ $b = 50°$ $c = 130°$ $d = 15°$
9. a) 74
   b) 10.75
10. 1.32 lbs
11. 7.5 km
12. 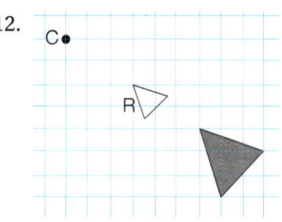
13. a) 122.5 m^2
    b) 63.6 cm^2
14. 4 hr 55 min
15. 52.5 m.p.h.
16. 239.5 miles
17. 5.2 m
18. 1 940 000 cm^3 (= 1940 l)
19. $l\sqrt{r^2+t^2}$, πr^2, and $2tl$ represent surface areas

Handling data
Quick test answers

Page 77 Collecting data

1.
Food type	Tally	Frequency

2. Make sure your questionnaire follows the guidance given on p. 77.

Page 79 Representing data

1. The angles for the pie chart are: Brown 120°, Auburn 60°, Blonde 90°, Black 90°
2. a) The frequencies for the heights are: $140 \leq h < 145 = 6$, $145 \leq h < 150 = 10$, $150 \leq h < 155 = 11$, $155 \leq h < 160 = 5$, $160 < h \leq 165 = 2$ b) 34 people   c) The frequency polygon should be plotted at the midpoints of the bars.

Page 81 Scatter diagrams and correlation

1. a) Positive b) Zero c) Negative d) Negative

Page 83 Averages 1

1. mean = 5; median = 4; mode = 4; range = 7
2. a) mean = 1.32 mins b) median = 1 c) mode = 0 d) range = 4

Page 85 Averages 2

1. a) 151.56 b) $150 \leq h < 155$

Page 87 Probability 1

1. Possible answers: I will get a 7 when I throw a die; I will get a 4 when I throw a coin.
2. a) $\frac{3}{9} = \frac{1}{3}$ b) $\frac{4}{9}$ c) 0
3. 240
4. $\frac{47}{200}$ (= 0.235)

Page 88 Probability 2

1. $\frac{7}{9}$
2. a)

		Die 1					
		1	2	3	4	5	6
Die 2	1	1	2	3	4	5	6
	2	2	4	6	8	10	12
	3	3	6	9	12	15	18
	4	4	8	12	16	20	24
	5	5	10	15	20	25	30
	6	6	12	18	24	30	36

b) $\frac{4}{36} = \frac{1}{9}$
c) 0

Page 90–91 Answers to practice questions

1. a)

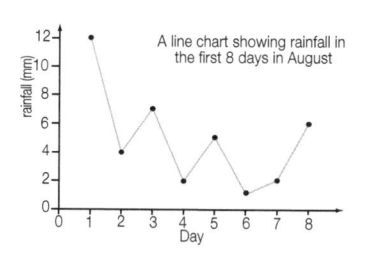

b) 4.875 mm

2.

Crisp flavour	No of students	Angle
Cheese & onion	7	105°
Salt & vinegar	10	150°
Beef	6	90°
Smokey bacon	1	15°

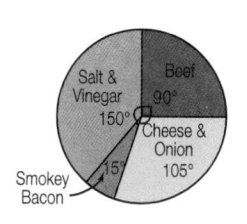

3. Mean = 3.125
   Median = 2.5
   Mode = 2
4. a) $\frac{3}{13}$ b) $\frac{6}{13}$ c) 0 d) $\frac{7}{13}$
5. 0.18
6. a)

	Under 13 yrs	13 yrs +	Totals
Boys	15	27	42
Girls	12	21	33
Total	27	48	75

b) 12 girls

7. a) 120° b) 8 hours c) 6 hours
8. 140 people
9. 42 races
10. 3.5
11. a)

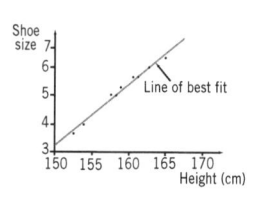

b) Positive correlation
c) See scatter diagram
d) 156 cm

12. a)

	2	4	6	8
3	6	12	18	24
5	10	20	30	40
5	10	20	30	40
7	14	28	42	56

b) $\frac{16}{16} = 1$
c) $\frac{2}{16} = \frac{1}{8}$

13. a) 50.7
    b) $50 \leq W < 55$

14. a)

Stem	Leaf
2	8 7 5
3	8 7 9 8
4	2 4 6
5	7 2 0 6

key: 3 | 6 means 36

Putting the leaves in order gives:

Stem	Leaf
2	5 7 8
3	7 8 8 9
4	2 4 6
5	0 2 6 7

b) (i) 38 (ii) 32

Index

acute angle 54
alternate angle 54
arc 48
area 70
axis of symmetry 52

base 26

capacity 66
centre of enlargement 60
chord 48
circumference 48, 71
common difference 38
compound interest 18
congruent 58
continuous data 76
continuous measure 68
conversion graph 45
coordinate 63
correlation 80
corresponding angle 54
cube number 4
cubic equation 36

decimal 12
  place 15
  point 12
denominator 10
density 69
diameter 48, 71
difference 8
digit 14
dimension 73
directed number 6
discrete data 76
discrete measure 68
divisor 9

edge 50
elevation 50
enlargement 58
equation 32, 35
estimating 22
exhaustive events 86
expanding brackets 32
expression 31

face 50
factorisation 33
factor 5
formula 31, 33
frequency 83
frequency polygon 79
function 33

gradient 41

highest common factor (HCF) 5
horizontal 40
hypotenuse 64
hypothesis 76

identity 33
imperial unit 66
improper fraction 10
income tax 19
index 26
inequality 39
integer 6
intercept 41

length 66
linear sequence 38
line graph 78
line of best fit 81
loci 62
locus 62
lowest common multiple
  (LCM) 5

mean 82
median 82
metric unit 66
mode 82
modal class 84

National Insurance 19
net 50
numerator 10

obtuse angle 54

percentage 16
perimeter 70
perpendicular bisector 62
pie chart 78
plane of symmetry 52
plan 50
polygon 49
power 26
prime number 5
prism 72
probability 86
product 9
proper fraction 10

qualitative 76
quantitative 76
quotient 9

radius 48, 71
range 82
ratio 24
reciprocal 4
recurring decimal 12
reflection 58, 61
reflective symmetry 52
reflex angle 54
remainder 9
rotation 58
rotational symmetry 52

sample space diagram 88
scale factor 60
sector 48
segment 48
significant figure 15
simple interest 18
simultaneous equation 36
speed 44, 69
square number 4
square root 64
stem and leaf diagram 85
subject of a formula 32
substitution 31
supplementary angle 54

tangent 48
term 30, 38
tessellation 55
translation 58
travel graph 44
trial and improvement 36
two-way table 88

vector 58
vertex 50
vertical 40
volume 72

weight 66

x-axis 63

y-axis 63